Farewell to Spring

MICHAEL MICHAUD

FAREWELL
to
SPRING

odyssey
International LLC

Cover: Detail from *The Abduction* by Paul Cézanne.
Cover design by Michael Michaud (Approved by C.K.)

Translations of the *Alcestis* of Euripides from the
1814 edition by R. Potter.

The author would like to acknowledge his debt to the
above-mentioned translation. A fair number of the poems
in the following work take their titles from the verses of
R. Potter. This appropriation was a late decision on the
author's part, and was merely intended to provide an
additional layer of context which can be discovered by a
parallel reading of the two texts.

Published by Odyssey International LLC
Salem, NH

ISBN 978-0-9837316-0-3

———

First edition

And so this is for you,
Amber,
Merah bahloo

Honest, lovely,
And very innocent,
Here is our little lovesong.

A shadow and a flutter on a branch,
And two bright eyes like sunlight on the grass below,
Sing together, not too innocently or too naively,
Love, love, love,
Is always better in the forest.

CAVEAT

These are not stories, but interpretations of stories; nor is this mythology, but only the bare echoes of those delightful tales; there is a logic, but of a scattered, by-nature-unclear character; and these are best flowed-with if they are read freely, but in order; by *freely* I mean without the expectation of narrative or closure, and by *in order* I mean the sequence in which they lie.

But anticipating undesirable frustration, I have provided *Clarifications*; truly, though, I would prefer them gone, and have these poems comprehended as bare as they are, never interrupted by any fumbling for a plot, always advancing, forgetting who did what or said what or why; . . . A nebulous cloud of tuneful images is always better than a blatant line of description and observation and event that sharpens to a small moral, and I would prefer that nothing is clearly linked to a system, or a history, or a plot; like life, let the interpretations be not anyone's but your own, and bind yourself only to the truest Clarifications, which are yours and I can never know.

(But in truth, the tales these *Clarifications* illuminate are all too well known to me, and so the poems are perhaps personally resonant in a way that they cannot, without a bit of explanation, be for the reader; I forget that you have not wandered with Endymion below the stars; but try to understand my disinterest in depicting the real details of the forests and the palaces, the heroes and the gods and the meadows; too many poets have done that work before me, and I therefore chose to illustrate only what a keen mind perhaps might not naturally choose to imagine, when led down the ruts of these heavily-trodden paths; so therefore I dislike and yet regard as necessary these Clarifications; . . . Isn't everything terribly reversible when we step away, even slightly, from our own impressions?)

BE OUR MINDS INTENT ON MORTAL THINGS

Delusion must know itself to be delusion;
Dreams become dreams only when we wake from them,
Else they're truth, and what they are is what we are, -
So we choose several truths and trust ourselves to them;
They may vanish, then we feel deluded; they may endure,
Never shattering our content, -

If all hope is delusion, how shall we find, when every dream
And variation of life has been exhausted, that last conceit
That cannot rely on death to lay it beyond disproof?

When delusion becomes necessity, even knowing itself as delusion,
Then will the hopeful garlands of love we gladly brow give way
To love as chains that bind us to eternity and endless lovers,
And life will become bearable only if it thus may go on changing,
And we will love only to kiss existence a while longer,
Till all joy pales and is not worth the pain of self-delusion.

CONTENTS

NOTE. The bracketed names indicate the poems' speakers.

I. FLAW

II. SYMPATHY

[Apollo] *Listen to my words, if you see reason in them.*
[Daidalos] *A soul's duration is its own eternity.*
[Daphne] *These things we know.*
[Apollo] *Well I know the circling bowl will waft thy spirits to bliss.*
[Admetos] *Oaths made for Love.*
[Voice] *The Trees. If life be dear to thee, it must be dear to all.*
[Daidalos] *Endymion.*
[Endymion] *On the humanity of solitude.*
[Voice] *The Streambed. Passing the bounds of life assigned by fate.*
[Daidalos] *Till age crept slowly on.*
[Voice] *The Wind. Not to do this would be the greatest wrong.*
[Apollo] *From eyes that never weep.*
[Voice] *The Mockingbird. She wishes to behold the radiance of the sun.*

III. SURRENDER

[Admetos] *Though the gifts of youth are mine.*
[Endymion] *Night. Aloofly he stands.*
[Daidalos] *Of dreams.*
[Glaucos] *His youth to all gave pleasure.*
[Daidalos] *Demophon.*
[Hylas, Heracles] *Sacred. Beautiful. Broad.*
[Orpheus] *The shroud of prescience.*
[Glaucos] *Wraith.*
[Endymion] *In fountain water she bath'd.*
[Hylas] *I saw you fondly coveting long life.*
[Heracles] *Is death alike, then, to the young and old?*
[Daidalos] *Such law from nature receiv'd I not.*
[Orpheus] *Abandonment. The bay.*
[Heracles] *Far from the hour of white horses.*
[Admetos] *To cross clear waters.*
[Orpheus] *Gazing into the flood.*
[Heracles] *Prayer. Cleansing of soil.*
[Orpheus] *Bathe them, composer, in sweetly-flowing water.*
[Admetos] *And let her go beneath the earth.*
[Heracles] *May no god be envious.*

IV. FAREWELL

[Icaros] *Buried thoughts.*
[Syrophanes] *Idos dolu, the appearance of grief.*
[Apollo] *Hyacinthos. What charm, what potent hand?*
[Hylas] *To wake from dreams.*
[Heracles] *Comfort in a night-bird.*
[Voice] *The Cuckoo. A solitary life estranged from joy.*
[Daidalos] *For to see a friend is grateful to the soul, come when he will.*
[Voices] *Songbirds. Bough-song hung upon a sleeping soul.*
[Zeus] *God speaks to the child.*
[Voice] *Thrush-song. Dream of an ideal ending.*
[Endymion] *The Asphodel Meadows.*
[Zeus] *Tartaros. Though an unreal vision of the night.*
[Endymion] *Thánatos.*
[Endymion] *Hypnos.*
[Heracles] *The Golden Cup of the Sun.*
[Daidalos] *Islands of the Blest.*
[Admetos] *The flow'ry wreath, and song that used to echo
               through my house.*
[Daidalos] *There await me till I die.*
[Icaros] *Then bid excessive grief farewell . . .*
[Endymion] *And visiting my dreams, delight me.*

Farewell to Spring

I

F L A W

CLARIFICATION *of* CONTEXT

FATHER, Daidalos, craftsman, and Icaros his little son, imprisoned in a tower above the sea; Icaros waking from dreams, to find his father examining river-reeds; how these will become wings; how this evokes the ancient fable of Pan and Syrinx;

God of the woods, musing, lone and melancholy, first glimpses the reclusive nymph Syrinx, finding her beautiful beyond all others; Syrinx, on her love of solitude; her flight from the amorous god, knowing his waywardness, his enchantments; his reasons for pursuing, hers for fleeing; lastly, how, in answer to her prayer, the nymph becomes a river-reed in the moment he grasps her, thus freeing her from his desires; and how his sighs, making lovely music through her hollow form, inspire him to create the flute;

The Argonauts, voyaging for the Golden Fleece, linger on an isolated coast for favorable winds; Hylas, ward of the great Heracles, binding a flute in the forest, muses on the music of Orpheus, how he sang in the last twilight; Orpheus observed singing by Telamon, who marvels at the effect of his music on the natural world; Orpheus' Moon Song, telling how the moon fell in love with the shepherd Endymion; Daidalos recalls for Icaros the story of the princess Europa, mother of Minos, how she was beguiled and kidnapped across the sea by the king of the gods in the guise of a bull;

The king Admetos, benevolent lord of Pherae, who long had withheld himself from the pains and vicissitudes of tender affection, chooses to marry the beautiful Alcestis, whom he loves; Heracles, waiting by the shore, calls to mind a strange feast, long ago, in the house of Admetos;

Daidalos recounts the story of King Minos and Queen Pasiphaë, the origins of the Minotaur, of their imprisonment; the craftsman's disgust with his own creations, his lament that his abilities enable him to satisfy wretched desires; and yet he realizes that without others' irrational impulses, he would never come to know his own depths.

[Daidalos]

He wakes.

It is this, my son: to remember;
To bear this flutter of a moment, this
Heartbeat-hope I wake you to, and you, waking,
Feel to the very sky . . . Out of dreaming, out of how I wake you now
From dreams to a dream I promise you is not,
As now you fall to the earth, and to me,
Is not a vision you must fall from;
And tho' your dreams release you
From precipices to the footing of life,
Know that these are wings, and are not stable;
Know also that you are not alone.

So we go now, off together, now to the
Brims of, wings hearts' fronds, rims of the sun,
Now without our eyes to guide us, reverie ride heaven-high,
Lost in a circle of light, we nimbuses round blinding delusion,
Feeling through colder and colder statures
For the warmer veins of the light that warmed us,
Dawns on dawns, from dreams to bonds.

[Icaros]

What he sees upon waking.

When nightingales sleep
Their small eyes close to fantasies
Of song and flight, - I know, for now am I,
O now a bird of a dreamer, beginning when I first perceived
That these were wings my father built to bear us across the sea;
He never told me his intentions, perhaps fearing to lift my hopes to the sky
Before he knew whether arms could truly take us there;
And yet he promised me that the flaws of his life would not always bind me
By the chains that were only meant for him,
And so one morning I woke to find him no longer adrift
In the pensive brood of deep deep thoughts,
But standing by the window measuring out reeds;
I saw him break away their plumes and study their length and suppleness,
Bend them to crescence in the sunlight and release them leaping
To flutter in the air, before seizing them in his hands, satisfied
With their sinuous grace; and when he saw me awake
And watching him, he said with a soft smile,

I was fortunate, Icaros, to dream of an old fable
I'd long forgotten, that told of how the reeds
That wave on riverbanks were first discovered
To possess within their slender frames a sweet sweet voice,
And how the wind of a lovelorn god's breath
Blowing his desperation through them
Caused their willowy pipes to sing so sadly
That he bound them together, to have them always near
To carry the voice of his sadness, that love had fled
To become this voice of loss.

[Pan]

God of the woods, his ennui. His first sight of her.

Does love have the power
To begin at once? Or does love only, truly,
Slowly grow, beyond what can be gathered
By a single glance?

I thought I knew every flower in the forest,
Yet somehow I passed over the fairest;
Many a dewy lip have I kissed of nymph
And mortal, and many a perfectly fair pair
Have been the feast of my regard; old am I,
Long past love's softer passions, and tho'
My dawn-rekindled youth will never brook
New harvests of lissom lovelies to pass me by,
I yet grow weary of so undeviating monotony
Of willing loveliness, so yielding
To everything I desire.

O yes, rings of trim ankles and silver feet
Were once my sole delight, and so they were
For a thousand thousand seasons, long before
The golden spires of men's cities rose against
The forest, I lived content with spotless beauty;
But the steady measure of endless days
Has beaten the charm from such earthy pleasures,
And I find I sit resignedly as the young nymphs dance
Below some misting falls among the lupine's purple spears,
And I cannot revel with them any longer,
Knowing the empty ends
Of all that love is not.

But now this morning I find you; you flash
Like a starling in the deep green dell;
Green huntress, you walk alone, unseen by most,
Not hoping to be seen or sought after
Or drawn by laughing revelers to their pleasant haunts;
But my eyes find you, and I have not known you
In the dances, or among the other daughters of the woods

As they play and sing, adorning their beauty
With small spread spouts of sweetly-breathing honeysuckle,
Or crimson-ringletting with teeming bryony
Their golden hair, or curling into little crowns
The wild grapes that darkly coil
Round dripping leaves in wispy strands,
They make themselves alluring . . .

I know you Syrinx, you shy nymph,
You purity of innocence, clarity, devotion, virtue;
I had not known you were so fair as you are,
Nor that such beauty could relinquish
What pleasures belong to beauty;
Yet I have heard you breathed of
Among the slender willows,
That you abide alone in the secret arbors
Of the densest valleys of the forest,
Abstaining from all of which eternal youth
Seems never quenched;

And I have grown sated, and now abstain
As you abstain, and try to make myself as pure
As you are, if wildness can crown its unrestraint
With a sublimer self-control; like some
Sun-drenched valley opening the dim dark forest
Through portalling limbs of shadowy cedar
You brightly seem to me, far off; and then,
As quickly as you shine, into the forest
You melt away.

[Syrinx]

Her loves and her indifferences.

O deep free cedar-raftered formlessness!
O loveliness without ideals to fetter you,
You immeasurable dream, mounting up
To thaw and shatter; not like men whose lives
Are spent in folly of changing devotions,
Nor like gods whose aimless endlessness
Makes devotion nothing; yet somewhere between them,
You forerunners of some vast purpose grow
Without a promise or an oath or a lie
To guide you, only the law of the forest.

Why does the woodbine kill his brother?
Is it malice? Or envy? Joy in ruin, or smothering love?
Or love only, selfless, for a both-loved light,
Makes one die, the other live? Willows weep not
That eve-sweet flowers must climb them to heaven,
Nor is he who callously climbs less virtuous
For making ladders of another;
Let introspection be their law,
Meditation more sinless and chaste and pure
Than a humanly-loving essence can rise to
To ponder itself, being bound, thus limited, by pity;
For to love is to consent to pity, consent to mercy,
Empathic fellowship with everything hatefully weak;
And to hate is not to remove oneself from the burdens of loving,
But to affect devotion, and then to heap oneself upon those
Who offer one their love they trustingly bestow, -
To hate is to lie, and if there are voices among
The things of the forest, they say that no truth
Is bent, certes, nor love misleading,
When the woodbine winds the willows to bondage.

Here is nothing dishonest, -
It is only the law of the forest.

Daughters of the woods, who sing like one another,
Dance, play, dream, love like one another, -

Do I defy you, am I arrogant, is my life contempt?
Is my happiness vexatious, that one so fair as I
Cannot be tempted by the lusts enchaining you?
You praise me, as I hear your songs
When they come to me on the ferry of the wind, -
And yet behind every general praise of pureness and clarity
Lies a mutual condescension toward the virtues acclaimed, -
The laughter of applause, the curiosity they, flocks,
For boredom deem delightful, is all their commendations amount to;
And so I care not, and that is scorn to them, is to ignore
Their love, to mock the love I owe them . . . So they dream
And I pass on, uncaring, and live apart, away from
Their answerless questions, that always turn their truths
On profits they will not question as supreme.

[Pan]

His approach. Her flight. His pursuit.

I hardly speak; she knows me;
Such diamonds have not swum with light
Before, and these but hardly, than she like mist
Along the rivulet's hemlocked bank unfurls
White vaporous limbs in flight . . .

O why did I begin to chase her?
Thought I 'twas best to assail her heart
Than win her slowly? I must seem mad
The way I follow her, and yet I am not driven, truly,
By lust; I think of pausing, of allowing her
To easily run away; but then I fear she may run on forever
And always elude me, always torment me
With a face I saw but once and was swept away by,
And then let go, without even a word to gather
What she was beyond her beauty.

[Syrinx]

Her defiance.

O green one, face of leaves,
You tainted one, dull lying one,
You think caprice is devotion?
You of the rugose heart, the anciently-bearded,
Broad-tendoned keeper of the woods, beyond years
Tho' glabrous yet of sinew and windswept lock, -
You call birds with your eyes and they come to you,
Cardinal arils of your eyes that call them down
To receive your fleshy nourishment, bright whispers
Of things most wonderful and strange; innocently they devour,
And ignorantly they broaden you everywhere, knowing only
That they are nourished and nourishment is enough,
And they trust you know the same.

You forsake simplicity, O sinuate one,
Whom nature has made a lance, - fly straight then,
To what you desire! Be not obtuse or elliptic,
Nor cordate like the heart, nor tangle as the tilt
And circularity of liana, loyalty renounced,
Vying with everything for the light.

What are you, to make of what is love to you,
Love to me? As tho' love is one thing only,
You speak as an old lover tells a lover young
All that love has made of *him*, as tho' a thing apart
From all that *he* has made of love;

But eyes rosettes protect their flower, and I,
Being loyal, fly straight to what is true for me, -
My heart I have not chastened wrongly, not given
To a blind devotion that keeps me apart from life,
Isolated in the folly of an ignorance that others
Deem themselves free of, simply because they commit to nothing, -
For love *is* a sacrifice: true lovers know this,
And that is their bond.

White dryad, you whisper, sweet haven of the mountains,
Have pity on a weak god adrift on seas illimitable,
Adrift until the shore of you brought me back to what is earth's horizon,
And made my heart beat motion again to the body that wilted
When it seemed to have felt all that a body can feel,
And then felt nothing at all, beyond the ends of indulgence;
O flower lonely on these heights, I have thought on you in every moment
Since first our bright corollas mingled in the early light,
And I wonder what there is up here that you rely on, -
In place of love as loved below, tell me what you've found
To love you better than a beating heart and a body parallel,
And a voice to echo delights and make subside the gloom of loneliness;
If there is nothing, I shall be there for you, if one
So once immodest as I can be the pity of one
So always incorruptible, that I might grow to find
What I never found in stormy freedom,
In your innocence and your virtue,
Something worthy of devotion.

You pretend to love what you desire, saying you come
With love and pity, as tho' to be some thing I lack in my isolation;
But never think that 'tis a blemish to the will of a clear being
To feel no pity when a weak thing stumbles upon its independence,
Nor fancy ever that I care to be desired; I flee now,
Knowing the strong impulse that will make you dream
To slowly win me over to love,
For tho' you ask how my love is different,
You'll think me not a lover, or a foolish one,
When you see my fidelity unadorned.

I hear your sweet whispers now, -
You know how to make a lover pause;
Another heart might be enticed by such a music,
But that is the choice of another heart;
Too young am I, and yet too fresh and simple
To succor the malaise of the worldly and disenchanted,
And I will not have my callow youth made weary
By the scorn and the doubt and the contempt of a jaded heart
That having fled what once it found so lovely now seeks
What lively fire of youth has flames enough for another.

[Pan]

His coaxings.

I have seen swallowtails courting like feathers
Borne upward on the wind, air-delicate, rhapsodic,
Loose and fluid and free . . .

There is a music in everything.
Wings make movement a song, tones plume
In the drop and rise, in the speech inweaving,
And fairness, however totaled, adds harmony
To the shift of things.

Love is flight.
Sun dies west, kills color to the creek
And the distant sound, silvers the low shard-moon, -
How fine is everything for love! how gently
The tiny water-striders skip the supple freshwater,
To quiver the waters like flesh!

O love, don't flee this, -
For how is the better part of life to go down continually
To a lone night, and colder dreams than beaming ash
Can dove-wing to a crescent gleam, and pearl vapor steam
Like vines to lock and curl the numb hard face of the moonlight,
The starlight, glazing loveless the face of delight?

Between harmony and flight, lovers dance, -
Never perfect, never ideal, never idyllic, never at peace,
Love makes them flee and circle, flee and circle, flee
And circle; let never that fear rest motionless
And complete, halted, cast in stone; may we always
Be dancing in the trail of one another, always be seeking
Or being sought, always be courting, and never be caught.

Swallowtails court like feathers on the wind, or a melody
Commingling among the spaces and bodies of the lovely world.
And whatever their music is to them, it is love to us.

[Syrinx]

Her appeal to the forest.

I am untouchably calm, my soul is, untouchably;
I am benumbed, and yet must go on feeling, must go on
Being felt . . .

Lifelessness is half the joy of slumber,
The other part, action without consequence;
Not only the pure flowing of imagination
Leaving the sodden verdure of a once-lushness
Drably heaped along the feebler flowing
Of the mind that wakes to the true fall;
Not only the valerian evening, sedating the mind's
Misery with far beastlier terrors whose swift extinction
Thorn-hardens lonely innocence's petal-softness;
No, no, not these . . . The world, not sleep, stirs these;

Do I happen to follow the pattern
Of what you desire? You may not say so,
But your love is self-regarding, how you follow me,
As tho' love is such license as to curb the path
Of a wholly different life, binding it to love
Like a disease that slowly eats away
The fragments of the heart that lasted
Beyond its lover's indulgences;

I have made for myself a lovelier life
Than the world could make for me . . .
You do not believe it? Deem me lonely, self-absorbed,
Deluded by solitude? No . . . There is no coexistence
Without bloodshed, even if only the heart bleeds unseen
Through slow years of mulish toleration . . . No, no,
There is no remedy for the silent odium
That churns below collective desire.

Proud, arrogant, condescending . . . I am none of these;
Aloof, perhaps; cold, indeed; indifferent, certainly;
And yet I take nothing, ask nothing, keep myself concealed . . .
I did not ask you to love me.

But now I see I am to be
A sacrifice; now I am desired, and all extraneous desire
Is fatal to an independent heart; O if only to somehow
Fade now into untouchability! Our kinship is only
Shape and outline, our minds are far divided . . .

So destroy me, what you can of me . . .
I am untouchably calm;
My roots are beneath.

[Pan]

Twilight. Mourns her passing. The flute.

Anon they (they are heavens) blush,
Yes they blush, leveled to the river and the lake,
Once cheeks that glassed the morning glow run off
To be an evening of mulberry skies,
Staining the red of their passion
Upon the waters that alike retreat.

They were heavens, and heavens are,
And I grasp them, grasping reeds, -
This hair streams not so delicately now,
These arms flow less, now peel off ragged,
This body abrades me, being rough, tho' I heal,
And these legs seize now the earth, nor flee,
And sigh and sing beneath my heavy breaths
As I shake them gently, releasing a lonely music;
I sigh, and they sigh too, but softer.

And is that all? Silence now, of a chase that ends
In nothing but myself, and I hold nothing but these reeds
That sigh more beautifully than I can sigh without them;
I pause, and their voices end; I cry out, and they choir;
Yes, this is all, this is all, and that is fine.

O for tears! For a few tears to soften
This staunch immortal flesh not inured to loss!
Tears are oceans, and tho' two small eyes
Weeping in a sea of beauty may seem incongruous
With the vast ponderous ends of the world
Around them, - world that sways
Undeigning to concern itself
With the tiny broken heart
That so little rain mends, - we'll not call
Pitiless what has no sense of hope and loss
And the changeful love that suffers and thrives
More on these than on rain or sun;
We'll rather call that cold remoteness
All that a lover is not.

And so these heavens blush, yes, they blush,
And I below them sigh on the tributary's brim,
And try to learn the thing she was
By playing on these stems that she became.

[Hylas]

The music beguiles.

I bind a flute among the rushes,
Halting the lower tips of hollow reeds
With bees' wax in shortening array,
Then tying them with sprigs and grasses
To make a line of mournful singers, -
I have in mind to mimic a melody
That strange poet sang last evening
As he sat upon the high balcony of the ship
And roused the mellow ropes of his lyre
To honeyed phrases he freed over us,
Like snow releasing from a cloud
And we the earth his verses drifted upon,
He somehow woke, like a true brother,
In each man, his most intimate longings.

How does he know my dreams to tell me them?
And whence this power to make real birds to fly his fancy?
It may be that he restrains, manacling to articulate sound
The freer mingling the world is, - or perhaps he amplifies,
Compounding the raw world to lovelier nuance,
To make us thereby love what is not like us, -
I know not, nor care to know, and no dull crowd
Of doubting thoughts these sweet notes
Shall unlovely and bone-bare
Dismiss from beguiling my heart.

[Telamon]

O that I had the pow'r.

Young, green, eyes of spring, so fully alive,
As all the life they hold and all they begin, -
A star is trembling over him, his tiara tall and gold
Twinkles in the grove, and he's loved by this stream
Whose bed he sings beside, whose dreams he brings
In melodies the flowers are dancing to,
Glad flutes of iridescent light lightheartedly playing
To his lyre's showers among them.

Violets violet earth's heaven he foots, -
He find them growths; he makes them violets;
So daisys he daisies, daffodils he daffodils, of bluebells
He makes the bluest bells; he makes love bleed
Or sleep in mist, he makes vines paint in blue blue day
The morning's glory; and everything rings
With every fondled cord, and with his words
That run like rivers now, now like bourns flow delicate,
Now sink down like rain or softer snow.

The winds are calm, they eddy warmly, flee
And circle, bearing melodies blithely off . . .
As tho' audacious to bear them over the world
Forever, through youth of yews and oaks' eld
They whisper and are lost, or level to
The purling of the stream whose waters leap
Like silver fish to catch the sun, and glory
In the love they pass, and roll, and roll on.

And what has not come dancing?
The forest bends around him, tilting
Cups and petals and boughs and shoots and fruits
Like eyes and ears that girt what loveliness delights them;
And even the tawny hermit thrush whose life is song
Stands by to listen, and there the mocker folded-winged
Keeps mute his variations, and there the cuckoo
Muffles both his moods; and spurs of alder, hazel, juniper bend,
Ridged with linnets, wrens and sparrows,

Larks and orioles and warblers, all awed to quietness
While he hymns, and even the tune-dumb forest of clatterers
Loads the branches to bask in fantasias of air
That only in dreams can they whistle in strains, -
O listen on, little birds, for there is no shame
In loving another's beauty.

I'll not intrude upon the love he shares with you;
Oft have I watched him trail his sacred suites
To a soft sad ending, and falling to noiseless peace
His charms released and the forest lifted away
In a million ovations of tweets and cries and sighs
And wingbeats that are not the forest's affected thanks
For a moment's pleasure, but songs recoupling his gift
Of threads of life.

He plays on, marshalling the great and the little,
Making little what is great, and great what is little,
Emboldening the low to the tall, and humbling the highest,
Mocking hatred with peaceful flowers gaily overcoming
Cruelty's tombs; he makes men of bears and owls, passions
Of shadowtails who hoard and sleep, and woodrats who build their houses
By the labor of many generations; and even the creeping serpent
Whose lidless eyes flicker in the grass gains more
Than sibilant voice when he wills him words
To frame his purpose;

His eyes are closed; never have I seen him sing
With his eyes open; sometimes I wonder if he knows
What he does, if his songs are as sweet to his own heart
As they are to mine, and I wonder if he has ever seen
What I see him do now to the forest and to the world
That but for this will never bow to human direction
Or gratify human prayer, no, not but for this,
A pleasant song.

He does not sing the love he finds in things, -
It is his songs that make them love.

[Orpheus]

Bow of the Argo. Night Song.

The moon is a beautiful maiden;
And the moon is a swan on the lake of the night;
And even she, tho' chaste and modest and most faithful
To her duty among the gods, once felt the pull of love, -

And as she glided high he glided low,
And by her life he knew his life,
And altho' distant, being a heaven away from his earth,
Yet in the pleading of his eyes she felt herself desired,
And she fell in love with him;

And diving down through starry heaven
On the wings of love, she circled low beside him
To watch him sleep, as only once through midnight stars
He slept, as once in every round cycle of noons and evenings
She bathed, unluminous, in the sea, and shook the shadows of the darkness
To radiant youth, and curving aloft over dark death to fan herself newly
Into crescence, gathered and veiled, of the beauty that grows and wanes,
The earliest gleams, and fell to earth beside him to hold him
For a moment in her eyes, and to love him with her eyes
But never to speak and so destroy his blissful rest;
Till steeping the stars' light with soft broad flames
Dawn summoned her, reluctant, to the sky.

[Admetos]

Never to pleasure more allied than grief.

Some day all of this will come to an end, all of this,
The trail of all life's thoughts, of all life's liveliest thoughts
Whose fading makes us wish them more secure
Before they've even left us, even together
With the possibility of far more embraces yet awaiting
Than have yet been spent, even so, the dread is there,
Dread of a sweet long farewell, like heaven to part with,
Like heaven on the earth, sweetening to the end,
Dread of holding, quickening, needing what will have to be lost,
Be lost as everything must be lost, even you, your youth,
Your innocence;

I may some day sit beside you as you die,
And that is more than I can bear.

[Daidalos]

Europa.

I. To Icaros, the story of Europa told.

See the shore, my boy, the golden shore;
See a princess on the golden sands;
See her golden curls, around a face divinely fair;
See her graceful walk, her modest gaze,
Her not-too-proudly-lifted eyes, which rest
As often on the sky as on the sand;
And shimmering her robes the soft wind,
And her maidens surround her, are dancing around her,
And lifting songs to the Sun, the Earth, and the Sea.

Gold greens beneath their feet as they dance
From shore to meadow, tall trees supplant the level strand,
And the bare sand gives up its golden purity
For the iridescent dazzling of many flowers
Mottling with color the grass' green.

Cheeks that blush, and eyes cavorting,
By life so far away rolling illuminated . . .
Girls, in youth, surrounded by a youthful world
Renewing itself so fragrantly, play like children
In the meadow, hardly mindful of the shadow-slant
Lengthening from sun's vermilion;

And he appears . . . Think of a white fabric blowing
Over hills, wind-bodied, far off, reckless in the tumble
Of its limbs, as free as the air beneath it;
And all this snowy flurry, so prominently radiant
Coming through the sleepy pastures of quiet gold,
Thrills them; their dances forgotten, they gaze on
Whatever phenomenon approaches . . .

       Suddenly,
He blows in among them, fair to the senses,
Like a balmy odorous breeze blows in calmly,
A great bull of immaculate white, who kneels

His great white form upon the flowers;

Nearly nightfall now, and the stars ice over
The chambers east, the dayfire is embers in the west;
Bafflingly fearless, they frolic around the mound of him,
Entranced, joyful beyond song or grasp.

II. To himself, unspoken.

She loved him,
For when he breathed
              There came to her the breath
                    Of far unfading fields,
Of the sea, and of the rose, folds spread, essence on the air,
                          Subsiding,
      In the bequeathal of itself dying
The loveliest of deaths.

                  She saw
Meadow on meadow rise, rising into hills on hills,
And slanting into valleys, sink away;
And all earth, tho' not directly, rose,
Crowned by mountaintops, thin peaks to the sun;

And she saw, contrarily,
All earth lapse away.
Out of eminence, obscurity;
Out of the vast, the fair, and the grand, the plain;
Out of the tall towered clay, all falling away,
          Less, less, less,
      And then the sea.

III. To Icaros, the story told.

Sun to the stars, and the blue world melts
Beyond the sea . . .
                He turns,
And to the moon rising lovely lows,

          Hee-a-lee-a-lee! Hoo-loo-loo-a-lee!
          Hoo-a-loo-hee, hoo-a-lee!

He sings,
And singing takes his way,
And sad those maidens are to see him go,
Saddest of all the long-listening daughter of the king
Whose eyes him follow till he sinks
Beneath the golden hillbrows,
And even the flutesong of his lowing
Falls away to the meadows . . .

Like a star reflected to a crescent in a gray eye,
The moon lifts pearl horns to the night-meadows . . .
Away to the palace, half in dreams, the princess nightlong
Floats in the dream-dale of vague enormous joy,
Hardly waking, allowing the morning to carry her off
To the sea, once more to the meadows, her maidens
Drawn dreamily behind her, as a spin-thread might be borne off
By a balloon of her own gossamer . . .

The twirl, curl of fingers, furl and unfurl
Of mist and voice, inhale and exhalation,
The far-off roll of the sea . . . And he appeared,
Seeming to grow out of the vapor the long grass
Exuded to the sky, and all at once he was around them,
Weaving a circle of white, so utterly, utterly,
Utterly beyond beautiful.

IV. To himself, unspoken.

Red roses' savor, and the dream was gone,
And left her where the meadows fade to the sea;
Those earth-brown eyes, that body heaven-white, his mantle,
Unearthly whiteness of a cloud, shoulders broad
Of a cloud-mountain, passive, peaceable, pensive,
Like a vague awareness or a vast anticipation
Of a answer not yet limned, limbed, locked in a concept;

And he was there, and they were there, -
He, something strange, wonderful, fearsome;
They, as they always were, emboldening, urging on,
Heartening on with sentiments that closed, enchanted,
On exquisiteness and splendor, their seeming good hearts,

Pure plain sincerity, honesty of pure open loveliness
That cannot but be virtue . . . So they danced, childlike,
Round the greatness of him as he seemed to kneel, obeisant,
Before her; doubts of a semblance flashed off him,
Like a voice from his eyes' eerie calm, absurd, unnatural,
Entrancing to the rim of terror, and yet so thrilling that abandon
Seemed the only way, this great beast come suddenly,
Brawn so tame and tender, so knowing of itself, so drawn to,
So loving of human beauty.

And then . . . O yes! the leap!
Defiance falls to faith, neglecting the acquiescence,
Calling it trust, calling it fealty, calling it longing;
Forgiving the eye that twinkles upon the submission,
Saying a tear welled rather, to bear her beauty's grace;
And they sang with their bell voices as he rose majestic,
Against their voices' charm beguiling with the flute of his,
And trotting round them wove the harmony to a pattern,
To a cadence, to a beat most soothing, soft and passive . . .

V. To Icaros, the story concluded.

. . . Till the music's peace sent them deeply into sleep,
And he, quietly, carrying, half in dreams, his fair object,
Down the golden sands made his way to the sea.

[Admetos]

Let not such fears disturb thee.

'Tis grim, lovely: Death must halve us,
Love must have us - to the parting - desperately near;
We must wonder the reason we consent to this, we who,
Devoted beyond all flaws love quite naturally,
Tho' quite unnaturally because we lead astray
Far more than our own hearts when we fabricate love's ends
That needs must crumble against the natural conclusions
Of everything that has ever been alive; we are
Far more than natural conclusions, far more
Than bole-wound weeds, climbing evergreens
Until our season wanes our silk to tatters.

Hold on to me, lovely, for Death must halve us,
Love must have us - to the breath-fall - unbearably longing;
To go together is better than to live completely apart,
This wish being not absurdity but great lucidity,
Mind's presence to remain in the moment of love;
To live on to other devotions we relinquish these,
These promises; and yet some say it is the way and the strength of life,
To live on beyond its losses, - resign, reconcile, long suffer;
Yet who would say this when his love is at hand?
O lovely I shall not whisper what I cannot live to complete;
We love, we hold, we suffer, and then we sleep.

O take my hand, lovely, for Death must halve us tomorrow,
But Love has us now.

[Daidalos]

Minos.

Minos, desiring the kingship of Crete, declared
That the kingdom was his by divine dispensation.
To prove his claim, he stood by the sea
And began a sacrifice to Poseidon, claiming
That whatever thing he wished for would be lifted
From the waves.

So he loudly prayed for a perfect bull to rise up,
That he, to the sea-god, might commit it to the flames.
And Poseidon sent a beautiful bull from the deep,
A spotless beast of heavenly brightness, roaring up,
Horns breaching the soft surf, charging through the slow tide
To bow before triumphant Minos, who knelt on the beach.

And Minos rose, knowing himself the king; the people knelt, -
And in his powerful pride he put his hand on the bull
And forgot the god who sent it; filling his eyes with the beauty of the
          creature,
He declared it too magnificent to be wasted in sacrifice,
Had it taken away to the fields, there as an ornament to be preserved,
And to Poseidon Minos lifted an ordinary oblation.

In fury shook and rolled the god of the sea;
He frenzied the mind of the peaceable beast, turned it wild,
And all along the countryside it raged, goring all who stepped
Ahead of its horns; it mangled herds of cattle into twisted heaps,
Tore up orchards, villages; indeed, so terrible did the beast become
That it seemed unopposable by human strength or device.

Not yet content, Poseidon redoubled his vengeance, and planted
In the mind of the queen, Pasiphaë, a desire for the savage creature.
To such a wild pitch rose her yearnings, that I, known to the queen
As craftsman of near-animate statues and nearly organic machines,
Was called upon in secrecy to compose a device by the genius of which
Might occur the consummation of her lust.

Too cunning, I carved a wooden cow, set it on hidden wheels,
Hollowed out a chamber within, and round it sowed a fresh hide;
And sealing Pasiphaë within, rolled the wanton queen-beast to a meadow
Wherein the terrible creature was known to frolic, and left it there. Not
        long thereafter,
The beast, bounding forward lustily, mounted and thrust his mad pleasure
        away.
So Pasiphaë was cured of her cravings, and gained the seed of a son.

In time she gave birth to a boy, and named him Asterios,
A boy born with the body of a boy, but the face of a bull,
And he was called the Minotaur; again was I commissioned,
And designed a maze of confusing ways to contain that wholly sadistic
        creature,
Who altho' human had the fury of his father in him, and a beastly mind
Not inclined to reason and peace, but to destruction.

[Heracles]

Drinking Song. A goblet wreath'd with ivy.

I.

Lovely is music
To the gods in heaven;
    Lovelier,
The full-souled dancing
To the harpist's melancholy rain;
      But loveliest
Of all things heard or seen by the gods who live forever,
The soul-blown flute-song of voice and heart together.

Here is the vessel;
The vessel brims with blood,
The blood of the earth; the nectar enters you
Like sadness, numbs you to the subtleties
Of bodily being, the cares that withhold
The thought-flow, the desire-flow, chain you to
Your saner self;

Holy, holy is the vine, and holiest he, the red-faced reveler,
Who of all deities most has given unto men the fullest foretaste
Of the sweet herenow, and the sweeter hereafter;
The earth's red liquid swirls with all of earthly wisdom and folly,
And to partake is to perceive the quiet end of sorrow
That is life's ending gift;

I drift between dreams, drunk with them,
Drunk with the desire to laugh at the seriousness
Of glory and majesty, love and desire,
Those brief little sparks that leap to their low little beds
Where long unbroken Time-extinguishing dreams will carry them
Swiftly to the other end of eternity . . .

O laughter, laughter! in laughter is life!
And in the memory of one or many sunlit hours
And the peace and quietness of soul drawn therefrom,
    Life's fair Meaning;

And I say there are . . .
                O yes there are yet many
        Loves and long hours of laugher
                        Brimmed with life,
And loveless laughless Death shall hold his peace;

O how I . . . O how I wish
That more would sing the less-obvious
Glad endings of things . . . Not only
More and better life is happiness,
But also is as lovely
The gradual acquiescence
To the fall.

II.

O how is it? . . . how is it
That the revels seem so ghostly
To those who slumber after wine?
The dancing, lovely, lively, deforms,
And embers fiendishly the soft red candlelight
In the eyes of the dancers whose spirit-swirl
Churns in the rush of wild music blended
With demented anthems of deluded love . . .

But when . . . when soft wings . . . but when
Soft wings beat gently, gently upon
Wine-drowned eyes, the frenzied soul
Descends out of passion to peace, becalmed
By luxury's fall to contemplation;
By carmine flood overlain and overwhelmed,
Now like a not-yet-soulless sober heart and sensing husk
Falling to the bottom of the immense impenetrable sea . . .

But then . . .
            Ah, yes, but then . . .
        But then amid the darkening smoke
                And the churning shadows,
        The bliss-fallen view the saturnalia
    From the height of their serenity;

Far fades the pageant, fades the color and the life;
Rise, dust;
        Fall, song;
    Weep, vine,
Your ruby soul to the dirt . . .

The futility of all this motion!
The swift upsurge, falling, soon falling away . . .

        But I think . . .
    Yes, yes, I think . . .
But I think it is better to give full wing to those
Wildest cravings within us, than to stifle ourselves
For fear of what we might become.

[Daidalos]

Of statues and machines.

I have made a thing that speaks to me;
Am I then an artist? Or what else is in
The fabrication of things that makes them have
Or not have value? Worth to others?
So creation must validate itself
By proving expedient to another's life?

I was called on to create an abomination,
And never seemed a thing so singularly vile
As this soft repulsive wish of the queen,
The pure white shining queen whose lovely
Little voice let loose allusions to a shockingly
Unnatural desire;

I coiled away, appalled;
In truth, I have not never fashioned ugly devices;
Cruel engines of conflict, petty lords' unmerited
Rock-top impunities, monuments to men better brought down
Than exalted; and yet I have tried withal to balance
The crueler needs of the world with what I think
Are truly noble aspirations: temples to the rightly-worshipped
Gods, their likenesses powerfully portrayed as deities
Descending sweepingly into a moment of living structure, -
Unstiffening the deadness from their godly limbs
I gave them natural movement, draped them with dazzling regalia,
Earth-colors, hung them with the treasures most befitting
Heavenly majesty; I flanked them with distinct creatures,
Gave back to them that portion of divinity their faculties
Contemplate, and having given earth heaven's livelier analogue,
Opened the thunder and forked fire of gods' eyes upon men . . .

Ah, but lightning oft
Disquiets, rarely chars
Ungodliness.

[Pasiphaë]

She tempts the bull.

I am the sunlight in a rainbow robe;
He does not feel the colors dance
On the brinks of his eyes? those silver eyes
Whose sea-gleam sinks me deeply into daydreams
Of a baffling exoticness, elusive allusive allure
Of a dawn-mist darkening the glass of the ocean,
Beautiful, mysterious, enchanting all at once.

I tempt unnoticed;
The beast he lusts for far off trots
Her animal loathsomeness
In disregard.

If,
To be desired,
I must deform myself
To be the beast he longs for,
I shall gladly suffer the change.

[Daidalos]

Pasiphaë.

Here is a queen.
She rests on meadowgrass
Among maidens' and flowers' innocence,
And seems so fair as they are indeed;
But her thoughts are not on maidens' songs nor flowers' fragrance,
But on this forest's Big Beast and the power of all big beasts . . .

She looks off to the warm distances . . .
Are these lovely queenly thoughts that draw her blue eyes so?
Or have they much of dusty writhing and the bull's groan?
She hides behind the heart's fair outline and lovely eyes
The lust of her soul.

This forest is deep and darkly woven,
And who can say what lurks therein in the shadows;
May be a god put this filth around her heart,
And indeed I feel that the flaw is not in her heart but in my own,
Knowing that in my power is the means to the consummation
Of a filthy deed and yet I do not withhold my hand . . .

I furrow, fumbling the mallet;
The soft wood barely quarrels with the gouge;
The demi-creature, half-perfect, perhaps more beautiful
Crude and coarse but carrying itself to a viler end
Than the beauty of its conception, creation,
Raw prospect, uncertain and immeasurable;
The ghostly balance of half a thing
Will always exceed the blatant expression
Of a mind's exploitation of itself,
Hope's consumption of itself
To complete one
Lonely possibility;

I somehow prefer the flaws that keep you useless,
That keep you art and not machine;
Art to most is useless, cannot by most be wielded
With any wide degree of power; but a machine

Is uncritical, undiscerning, blindly empowering,
Bolstering, shoring up weaknesses that godly long sight
Would never sanction;

Not even hollowed out yet, what are you?
Not a true beast, no, nor even truly the likeness of a beast,
But like some malformed collision of ideas you stand
Half-hewn and very beautiful, peeling swiftly toward
A dreadful purpose, bloom to the mallet's knocking,
Wreckage of so many lovelier theories, trials,
Fruitless endeavors and possibilities scorned.

II

S Y M P A T H Y

CLARIFICATION *of* CONTEXT

ENDYMION, beautiful youth, shepherd, lone in the wilderness; how he came to love his solitude; how he came to love the night; how he cast off the daylight by sleeping below the earth, only to emerge at dusk; his ode to the turnings of the moon; how the moon fell in love with him;

The completion of the wings; the hesitation of Daidalos; their escape across the sea;

Apollo, in love with Daphne, a chaste nymph, sings her heavenly songs to win her heart; how she spurns him, unwilling to devote to love; how, desperate, he chases her; how she, fleeing, prays to the earth, and becomes a laurel tree;

How Daidalos finds Icaros no longer in his trail; how he finds feathers on the waves;

King Admetos holds Alcestis in his arms as she passes into death; how the god Apollo had granted the king a stay on death, could he find another to die in his place; how none came forth when the king became ill; how Alcestis gave herself for him; how her oath is irrevocable, as all oaths are, when made for love; how the king must watch her gradually die;

The king wanders in the forest; his thoughts on death; how his thoughts drift on various objects, and what they say to him; Apollo weeps for love and immortality.

[Endymion]

Ode. Justly do I hate this stranger then, who came amidst our grief.

I. New Moon

Not for the furthest reach of mind or hand
Nor starry benevolent arms of heaven dove-like lowering
To raise men's hearts, pitying them, making void their vain struggles
And the lessons of Life and the World, -

Men shall not make men out of heaven's stars,
Nor shall heaven make stars out of men,
And tho' the love of Man for Man sows in our hearts
Beautiful longings for spring's endurance
On blessed islands of eternal human love,
We must at last concede that no god will mediate
Our dreams to nature, and cancel rains and winters
And witherings to leave us holding
Life's pleasantries forever;

Often men find sympathy in nature
Only when they look on what is obviously beautiful,
And men find goodness in Life and Men when they gaze only
On fragrant moments of Men and Life, -
And somehow they find in nature
A Hand to preserve them;
In bird's evening melody they hear a call to love's perseverance,
And no voice or music of the world will ever say to them
That God is indifferent to Love, -

Unbound to Love, men rely on Reason, and discover in the certainty
Of natural observation, the comfort of recurring truths;
But Love is a vine, and when it wraps our unsuspecting hearts we find
Our need for reason shattered by Love's call to beauty, and meaningful
        folly,
And we see that what is true for God
Will never be true for men.

II. Crescent Moon

O has ever so silver
        A sliver of moon
    Mounted so cold
            An ice-blue day's end
        Fading glow
                Of bluebell on lily-white
                    Luminous upland plain
                            Of open sky?

Low moon, you lovely woman, and I
In the forest below, gaze on the twined trees,
The lonely flower lightly furled . . .
Unfurl now, O Liana, unfurl, unfurl . . .

            Liana, Liana,
        You are the opening moon . . .
You bride, spinning in your snowy gown, glow
In the glades of the night, dancer of an evening . . .
You shall be wed by the dusk, shortly love,
And die despondent when the harsh dawn carries off
The stars from your eyes . . .

            No tears, O Liana,
Will you weep to the cruel day who dries them,
Hardening you to love's vacillations which all beings
That choose to endure as things pass away
Must bear . . . Allow never the convolutions you were born from
To knot you into their misery and the misery they cause;
You were not formed because they willed it, and to their evils
Are not bound;

But see how their green arms hold you as you pirouette,
The swarms of them, how they tangle, hungry, desirous,
Teeming over everything mountable, as thirsting they ruin
The ladders they climb?

It is: the disorder of our perceptions;
And I feel it is not shameful to flee the convolutions
Of what is designed to flower nothing, only tangle;

For tangling has never been my heart's desire;

O Liana, I want you not to be a part of them,
To be some different soul, not complicit with their hateful hunger,
Some rare great star that funneled through their decadence
To surge free for one distinct evening of tremendous beauty,
So die in triumph;

That true beauty as you are, O Liana,
Might release, occasionally, from the vulgar commonplace,
Is a thought I can hardly bear, -
And I tremble at the fancy (tho' I now begin
To think it true), that we are not what we are,
But what we flower.

III. First Quarter

City on the shore, far off,
Beyond the deep of dreams . . .
O why, night by night, do I fly to you,
Lone below the big-bellied sail
Of the vessel of myself, up the massive sway
Of the swells that roll and crash in strange disorder
Below the clouded stars?

The sea's arms yearn
To grasp the veils of the moon . . .
They lift like dark titanic bodies
Rising above death's earthy gulfs of sable abyss
Their black-haired black-eyed raven shadows,
Then roll beyond me . . .
Each growing head of crowning foam
I ride to the valleys of heavenly sparks,
And very distant spy this far-off city
In a moment of light . . .

The charred mists darken
The shadow of the shore, that might
On calmer nights have shown sierras of swarthy mountains
To the blue of a midnight sky . . . Yet through the gloom
These far lights glow, and reach their havening arms

Of fired gold across the waters,
That waver them as they beckon . . .

No mystery 'mid storms why I'm drawn to them;
And yet I blink and the sea is calm, the breezes warm,
The stars unshroud; and still I find my yearnings shoreward,
Far over the massive calm to the heart of this strange and luminous
City of men, that yet abhors me as I'm lured to the warmth
The veins of it offer . . .

But can you tell me why, O lights, I love you?
Why this impossible need pulls my tears
Toward it, until I feel that I have missed some great beauty
In what is common, communal, accepted by the world,
As tho' I am some fool to fight the clearest sentiments,
The palpable, the blatant, the evident joys
That make life among others more agreeable
Than to spend my span of days only among myself;
O this impulse! Craving, compulsion, inclination,
Tending me toward the fondness of shared feeling,
Casting the brood of contemplation and meditation
Into a selfish useless vain solipsistic light,
Or rather half-light, or haze, to be cleared up
By shouldering a share of the life that is a broader life
Than a single life;

Is my youth what makes me love and hate the familiar?
Is this romance, that I love myself and the night?
Or do I see how prudence perceives
The absurdity of wisdom in society, how it concedes
To a brute usefulness, dispensing with the subtler beatitudes
That once were the ends of the soul? Am I too much
Bound to the earth that I fear to mix myself
With a dreamless eternity, and thereby lose myself,
Myself whom still I love?

But all that draws a tear is not essential,
All that kills with pity murders nonetheless;
I am not a duration, and they shall not endure
Beyond my falling, nothing of nature stand
Beyond my falling; all appeals to coexistence survive

Until I turn my eyes, my voice, sailing off from every other . . .

O dim city! O virtuous-seeming white-lighted sanctuary of men!
O agreement, consolation, friendship, comfort, peace,
And everything lone minds cannot own or revel in!
O temptation to the absorption of so-various experience!
This has the look of death, this broad assimilation
Of everything I singly am with everything apart from myself,
And I see nothing desirable in this;

O yes I want you, but only from afar, -
'Tis best you stay a distant light.

IV. Waxing Gibbous

You, broad of body, branch of the earth,
Gripper of ends and bowels, temples and crown above,
Between fear most buried and the sprawl of wild need
I find you firm, the navel of many things too awful
And too free, great strands, fibers of you,
Diving lengthening tendons arms of you, -
My dread goes down, faith ascends
A body so divided, -
So the stars grow near;

I say to you: Tell me nothing
Of Fate, no, nor of gods' devisings,
Nor make little of men's wills in the shaping
Of men's endeavors; I would have men
Grapple with their destinies in the sunshine,
Not in the obscuring loom of an unknown god's
Shadow, whose darkness breaks the daylight to a mingling
Of brightness and shade, and clouds the clear light
That once fell fully on the motions of all things . . .

Enough then! Enough! I make you a metaphor: for I,
I thought the sun was low in the sky, but it was only
Behind a cloud, I say, say to myself, as others cannot
Tell me so I tell myself that life is only life, death
Is only death and the end of living, and still within this limn
A Moral and a Meaning as fair as the fair conceit

That death is life and life is only the beginning . . .

O the ostensibly profound, the charlatan sacred,
Would do best to crack their gilded rounds
And have their dome be glittering sky!
From thence are prayers to God not wafted indirectly,
The prayerful breathing not the incense smoke
And the heat of a candle's flame, but the breath
Of God as they pray;
                    And their prayers being free
            May freely die among the sunlit trees
And the tall warm hills that ripple in a passing breeze;
                    As ever,
            The truest creed proclaims,
That neither God nor godliness may be bound by human decrees,
Nor shall the mortal sight of God degenerate
When by small men great God is limned,
And tho' before the mockery of divine authority
Men may waver, God is glorious because He is natural,
And never may men glorify nor supersede
                            Nor diminish
                The freedom that is He.

Some say that there is nothing without Man;
That Man is alone, and apart from all things;
They say his soul gives him dominion,
Exalts him over oceans and mountaintops
And endless plains of trees;
They say there is a Greatest Soul,
Who in His love and perfect genius was led
To lower His immortal image to the clay;
And they say that this fair earth is a proving ground,
Or else a vision, a fair or foul dream, -
And they wonder: to what end this fair illusion?
To enlighten, purify, or deceive? Why have we men
Our godlike Will and Reason, if not from God came we?

O how narrow is their vision who weep not
When the vast sun sets, who standing small
On some great peak above the greater ocean
Beneath the golden vault that strides the world feel not

That no god like a craftsman made them,
          Heart, limb, and brain,
To satisfy some aesthetic ambition;
They narrow God who think He stands apart,
Who dream Him less than everything, and we,
More than grains of sand beneath His endless sea.

V. Full Moon

It is men's terrible tendency
To revere what confounds them;
It is the blaring day, that bares blatantly
The intricate earth; it is a great blind eye
Darkening the mind with light;
It is something softly singing
In the emerald and diamond depths
Of the lovely world; it is beyond doubt,
Beyond demonstration, a voice eternal, a voice unchanging;
And yet we cannot trust a heaven that vaguely wafts to us,
However fragrantly it scents the breeze;

Fairest at the first and last,
High sky, full from heaven, falls
And is reflected fully, and the answer coming voiceless
In the skyward growth, in the folded fully unfurling,
In the spring and swell, in the changeably opaline
High and low heavens of the earth, always wavering,
Here, now, for a moment, and then the moment going
Newly uttering the Now and Here.

Pale and infinite blue somehow bends; before this
Blue, brown branches wave in wind, green leaves
On them, red berries, birds among these, hills of
Green-golden grass that lift like waving flames
To brush the tall sun shining . . .
And the wind bends all this, even the sky
Ashift in wind with sailing clouds is changing;
And there is no real silence nor solitude,
Too much is living, too much sings, flutters,
And is alive; you may say that when unclouded
Yon blue sweep no less serenely unfolds

Than star-surrounded moon and fields of the deepest dye;
Say that all the color of the world
Melts into the dimday afterglowing afterlight, on into
The deep-toned full darkness wherein shines not
The world in rainbowed riot of infinite colors,
But is the dancing only of pure-white light
Between the shadows, a blackened world unspectrumed,
Reft of peacocked Beauty's lively play;

Truly the light is sweet, and the shining world
Of all things most beautiful to gaze upon,
When the wandering eye is met by the colors of the meadow,
And the trees rained upon by spectral sunbeams shattered
By the leaves, and the stream translucent to the golden bed
Plays on the shining stones flows on undimmed;
When river, lake and sea burn blue-golden
And the white and purple showers dip from the boughs on the bank
And ripple the still silver when a small breeze waves them;
When the honey-blond beaches bask beneath cliff and forest,
And amber, topaz, beige, die into the foam-flecked waves;
And the clouds not colorless, but simply fair, float by
Pure-white, snow-white, lily-white, and between them
The sky of massive blue, cyaneous, glowing, sweepingly, billowingly,
Deeply deeply blue, and the Sun of all things brightest, hence
The only colorless thing, tho' called golden for the golden things
Which mirror it: the sunflower and the dandelion,
Primrose and daffodil, the golden bursts
Of the goldenrod;

The aurulent, the low-lobed, the sunshine-yellow,
The green-golden light on leaves, leaves on trees,
Trees on hills, hills on seas, the drawing down
To the still-blue western sky, where still the faded sun
Glows lightly, lightly azuring the vaulted heights, the depths,
The valleys full of stars . . .

Enough! Enough!
I run away with it!
O for the deeper sky!
The sweet moon dear to me,
The silence, the leaping stars!

I found the night and the night was freedom,
And the night was naked and a shedding of semblance,
And the night was honest
And never lied;

Not out of understanding;
Not love as humans love;
Not sympathy and sacrifice and self-deception;
Not a single serious impossible promise;

What these stars bequeath to my imagination
Is the only link between myself and all without,
And is undoubtedly the very hand of God.

VI. Waning Gibbous

Locked in deathless deliberation,
The dead ones' eternal slumber mocks life's dream
Of Forever's freedom, -
So are the dead ones gone to a heaven of blissful dreams,
Futilely, mindlessly, senselessly immortal,
Unlike the Living, who altho' made foolish and rash
By the hungers and pastimes of living, nonetheless retain
That power to Will and thereby liberate themselves
From the nightmare of infinite possibility, -

Alas for the lover in me,
Who loves and pities the frail impotence of men's decisions,
That I pity and love, but cannot admire, fools' sufferings;
Nor can I admire the station of the gods, who tho' eternal,
Must live and will at the pace of human variability,
To whom they sacrifice by loving them
Their eternal godliness;

For men will prod eternity to see if it sleeps,
And if it claws at them they fear its wrath in provocation,
And if it wakes and eyes them serenely, they love the calmness of the beast,
But if it does not stir after many proddings, they drag it out
And flaunt to others the brute they've slain;
This circle of hatred swings between heaven and earth,
Compelling men to hate their gods for the prudence

Their gods demand from them, and gods to ripen
To a weary disdain for their children below,
Whose constant cries demand that Father and Mother
Fall to them continually from their contemplations in heaven, -
Truly all is above as it is below:
It is the sympathy of mothers and the expectation of fathers
And the crude ambition of sons and the crass rebelliousness of daughters, -
And how I pity the gods who must waste their meditations
On the vanity of men, and waste eternal hours
Drawing down destinies on men's presumptions,
Finding that men simply grow again, and the new men
Have learned nothing from their fathers, whose folly, as they watched,
Shattered their bliss to misery;

How tidelike must seem the unceasing generations
Of petty stupid men, who live too briefly and too blindly
To ponder anything eternal, and pass on only misapprehensions and fears
To their progeny, whose reverence for the false wisdom of their forebears
Is borne out of a foolish respect for what old in men,
When they rather should love and cherish only what flows
Purely through the world, never reverencing love blindly,
And never bowing with a broken heart to what others say is true,
And never too timid to outlie outlier-condemning worships,
And never trembling at the gates of loneliness, boldness failing,
As others cannot love them, thus unable
To love themselves.

VII. Last Quarter

Here is prayer:

Starlight the leaning Mother skys, candling me calm,
Fear-freed, companioned by everything,
Daylighting elms' dusk from growing
The demons mind makes of shadows,
Mid-storm, mid-ocean, composing peace,
The benevolent twinship laughingly marking
Of Death and Sleep.

O love! O Moon my love!
Leave me never, my loveliest light,

Light I live only to see you lift
And swing the sky,
Not lost in the ocean of the day,
But fairest amid lesser fairs
That rim and garland you, -
Thus you smile to me,
Filling me with the calmness
Of truly enduring beauty, -
O I love you, O Moon my love!

World of sleepers, sleep on! Cast my lover
One or two dumb glances in a blind lifetime,
And boast you know a beauty better than she;
I don't care to listen any longer; the law of beauty
Is opinion among you, pinioning the grander world
Whose quiet voice is drowned by so many men
Shouting their faith in the importance of themselves, -

The Moon tangled in the birches - that is beauty;
Stars, from their tremendous heights, blinking
In the mist of the waves that break and fizzle
Whitely on the black shore - that is beautiful;
Alder masts that wave their shadowy sails
To a lightless oblivion - beauty, that is beauty;
Olive calyxes that widen their fruition
To the dewy deepness beyond the sun - beauty;
Streamlets hissing, breathing, whispering
Beyond the sight of eyes, deep in the grove,
Under the sacred darkness that carries their voices
To the mind, flashing there their diamond waters -
And they are beautiful;

Why will never the world return our love? they cry
When at the mercy of it, as tho' all love
Were obediently symbiotic.
But who has a heart, the man or the sea?
O forget not what belongs to the heart,
You who would frame yourselves in what is heartless!
The fancy may prosper while you seem to grip
The distant power, and yet you voyage near
And the power grips *you*, and is not friendly at all

To the flattering love you dreamt was that which made it move.
But the power of the sea is not the soul of the sea,
Or not, at least, as men define their souls,
For 'tis innocence that divides us; -
To be as the world is is not to be as men are,
As men define their beauty by everything
Without themselves, while the world suffices
On the beauty it contains within.

O love! O Moon my love!
O faithful fount defining a perfect faith!
By rising up you dignify the walls of my soul
And make me look for lovers in things more constant
Than human hearts. You need not love me,
You who cannot love the way I love;
All I wish is that you shine.
No dream is less a girl to love me,
Than if I found whom most my heart desires;
Your love is silver light, but there is more to you, -
May I know you better through myself.
O how I love you, O Moon my love!

VIII. Waning Crescent

Eyes pale and are closed by the hands of another,
Souls scatter in the wind,
And every hill shall come to vault
Some doused lover,
Whose smolder brought him finally
To his end.

O how many men may lie beneath this meadow floor!
How forgotten! How utterly forgotten,
Lost, unwritten, unrecorded, unremembered!
I climb these hills, grassed and flowered
And bursting at the crown with colossal trees,
And I know not what these barrows signify, -
Monuments, are they, to the dead within them?
Earth's tribute of endless seasons poured forth
In stalk and shoot of campion and white sweet clover
In their leap and murmur, sweet savor and dancing white?

Should I feel a kinship with the unknown dead any more than I feel
That these truly are my brothers whose dark unmoving limbs dissolve
Perhaps not deeply beneath my feet? Tell me, O hills, if you know,
What speaks more to the presently living
Than the presently alive?

O yes it may be true that the husks of those once living
Lie inhumed in many a meadow, or loved hill or vale,
And it may be true that after one lone cycle of the seasons
The long grass grew and grew over them, and overgrew and brushed away
The signs that men were there;
And it may be true that more went into the meadow,
More lifeless skins were locked away in slope and swale
And even the memory of the dead ones fell away;
And it may be true that the earth is fed
These once-beautiful minds and voices
Only to make nothing of them, - rather to abolish them,
Their beauty, broadness, reflection, insight, invention, all they were, -
And so the dead are mourned, God given sympathy,
And life's end feared without His heaven.

But must we lie so deliberately to ourselves?
And why is the true state of things insufficient?
As things are, I deem our place
Within the order of a godless world
Is infinitely lovely . . .

My eyes see a shrine to the Beautiful.
The beauty of the world fountains from
The liberated minds of the dead, whose deaths discharge
Worlds of Thought and Will upon the living, -
So the tree grows out of the man who most in life
Sought to know the beauty of it, and the ocean steps
To the shore, drawn by those who loved the dunes
And now dwell within them, and ebbs away, away to the deep,
Toward the sea-dreams of all ocean-lovers whose beds are now
The deepest beds, and from the high sands the sea oats
Wave tribute of curving plumes to the depths that swallow souls,
(For not till a man was drowned in the sea did the sea have any meaning),
And then there are these hills of oaks whose broad roots gush
From the hearts of men whose graves are hills

Because they loved the hills,
And the hills slope down to the meadows
Wherein those lovers of flowers rare and wild
Now give forth from ruptured forms
A new spring's color and spray,
And high above them, the sun and silver moon
Incline, burn and shimmer, and decay, drifted
On day-blue and beautiful clouds and stars' deep eternity
Together with the sweep of ghosts' eyes that look on heaven
From the headlands whose grass they loved
To lay upon on summer eves;

Ah, but wait now, young heart, -
Don't sing too much of truth,
Knowing you know little, but listen,
And hear what comes . . .

The forest whispers, the trees, faintly, speak, -
In leaf's flutter and song-uttering bird and sway of grass and flower
Some aspect of Man's character is somehow intimated, somehow evoked;
                    O beautiful world!
              And worlds beyond you!
Are you what men become when life leaves them?
When the sole beauty of this fond mosaic that men call Life
                    And which they dream around themselves
Dissolves in death when the soul is forced
                 To accept the apathy
                            Of what is tangibly and definitely True?
And out of life's joy and unpredictability,
Does the soul not die out of sadness into the Truth?

If so,
We have little to fear from death,
Other than the loss of ourselves.
And yet we cannot allow death to make nothing of life,
Nor can we delude ourselves with false hopes
We know we cannot more then half-believe;
Our solace, rather, lies timidly, moon in a cloud,
And men call: Doubt.
Only once a man has put aside his smallest fears
And come to cherish above all things that *he* gives divinity

To all that seems to him Divine, - only then,
In the strength of all that he has, and the greater strength
Of all that he has lost will he learn to accept
That no god would be foolish enough
To drown the beauty of a woundable soul in too much bliss.
Our dreams yearn out of us, and when the last frail foolish impulse
For a judging God has died in the last soul,
Only for Doubt will men carry on dreaming.

IX. New Moon

You, you pale dawn, rupturing the bloodless east,
If always you could lift me with cherry blossom arms
To the peace of dreams, I would love you as the rising doors of bliss
Opening my heart to rapture! If never you would knock against
The gently fallen leaves lidding these twin iris blooms
Wherethrough intrudes the light of the world,
I would love you as the tender veins
Fastening my heart to the true vessel
Wherefrom, and through, and to,
        Flows life, -
And if never the moon would abandon even one evening of stars,
I think that I would never need to endure the day
To achieve the night.

This deep grotto, domed with oaks' hidden broadness
Of ancient roots twining the dark earth they drink upward
To the light, wombs the fragile dreams that nurture my heart;
And there, through a fracture in the rocks, through the arms
Of this first heaven of vaulting oaks, the fair stars smiling down
Out of clear blue eyes and full-blooded auburn glances
Romance my mind with warm-hearted floods
Of evening's passion . . .

Emerging to meet them, I find the thin rim of the young moon
Low upon the heights tiaraed with silver light, and whisper
To the swelling heart within my dark frame climbing,
Once more, nascent lover, with you,
Love arrives.

[Apollo]

He charms her from afar.

I love, so am a lover,
And you are my beloved.
Is there shame in being beloved?
Or shame in being that kind of beauty
Your lover craves? But you disdain beauty,
Yet therein are beautiful, and yet fear that love,
Even true, will weep when beauty weeps, and desire
Beauty afresh, as tho' thus love would freshen too;

You, whose hazel eyes hold four seasons,
Dream only you can love yourself with a love
That grows as you decline, loving, pretty, that youth
Sang through you once and still is singing, but now is blent
With all you grew to be.

Lay, dove, lay your fears of broken trust,
Of abandonment's dissuasion, from your heart, -
Your love is best to me because it will not lower you
To being only what I desire, keeping you nobler than some
Obsequious fantasy the illusion of our love depends upon, that when,
As it must were I so vain, my lust would tire of your shape to allay my
          pleasure,
My love and yours, being beneath my mercy, would fail;

Before love, much divides us,
And let love never divide us less, no, never,
Because I want you as you are, never as you deem
I want you to be, and I want your separate soul to clash
With mine, that we'll together make us other than we thought we'd be,
Before we knew how love remakes us;

Do you fear me because I chase you?
Rather I strain because I fear to lose you,
And I pursue because my love has begotten fear
Within that heart I dreamt might dream I've come to allay
Its fears, - but you flee what seems hot blood in these veins,
Conflating honest passion with thieving prurience,

And think shoal appetites lengthen out my fingertips
To brush your streaming hair . . .

But lust is shallow - I know this - and desire is a passing fair,
And we learn only what we presently are
From what inflames us;

        O desire!
We cannot always have what we desire;
True of moments, but everything we look for
Time finds for us, and that which we think we want
Thus changes, as we're grown by what we suffer;
By what loves us and does not love us
Does what we truly should love
Become clear.

[Daidalos]

The Laurel.

Only once he held his lovely,
Only felt her heart one moment course
The tender flow of life;

And lowering the sunlight of his eyes
To the delta of the laurel in his arms,
He felt fade away like ebbing bells his hope
Of many seasons of love, and saw her
Spread away and scatter above him
Into boughs and branches and leaves . . .
They fluttered once and she was gone.

As men's hearts break for vanished love,
A man would weep, - but he with one fresh loss
Deepening the winter in his ageless heart,
Clung for a desperate moment to what still
In the young tender tree seemed like a young tender woman;
And tho' he knew love's promise once more had fled forever,
He clung beyond hope and reason beneath
The whispering crown of the bay, and felt
How deeply he had lost, that only once
He held his lovely, and she had chosen death
Before his love.

[Apollo]

Listen to my words, if you see reason in them.

O gentlier pulsing tenderest heart
Each rhythm in the leafing wood,
Tell me why you fled my kiss, - why, young dove,
You ribboned the woven woods with ivory flight
From a golden lover, love songs fled of a golden thrush
Who sang not one harsh note of reckless lust, but tender songs
Timed to your timorous heart, hoping to lure your heart
Too timid to love from this prison of chaste folly
That fears love as a weakness, and love as a conquering,
Till you see that love is the bliss of the union
Of the world you're held by
To the world you hold.

Tell me what in the world is worthy of worship
Even to the end of life, that withholding your desires
From the pleasures of sensual love
Stiffens your soft flesh to cold boughs,
Untender to my warm embrace?
Why flee to the fragile hours of life,
To the summers and autumns of the descent of living,
And the pale winters extinguishing the fires
Of beauty and passion and lust?

Fled to this, you have no more to flee, -
Out of voice, out of mind, out of deed,
Once a girl, now only
A tree.

[Daidalos]

A soul's duration is its own eternity.

Heaven has roots, and those are the sky,
And feeling down for springs they nourish heaven with earth,
And earth too, having arms to nourish it, spreads them
Into the blending ocean of all formlessness
And draws so many fragments up to make them
Symmetry and to make them Beauty
And to make them Life, -
So men shoulder their passions
Between chaos and heaven's order,
Calming wild lawlessness
To form and grace;

And so gods learn of love and beauty;
To heaven they've taken our youth's offerings
And the children of our experience,
And thus accepting them have made them standards
By which we balance what we are to what's supreme;
And so gods learn what things are noble, loving them
To make them godly, for if men did not
Love before them, and die in the name of love,
They would not know what things are worth upholding,
When a soul cannot sustain itself and be itself forever;

For not a thousand years of changeless spring
Can teach what beauty is, removal never suffering love through
The compromises that make love true, and so they'll search
For what their own hearts long for, so as they grow intricate in years
Aloofly they'll scorn how love deludes hearts to sacrifice,
When what we give our hearts to too soon is gone,
And all was vain because we're nothing again;

But in the wake of love, remembrance flowers;
So sovenaunce is love's fountain;

And so why weep, bright god, for one laurel?
Some day your eyes will find her gracing another forest,
Or nearly her, and time will make your heart amenable

To her eyes' first greeting glance, the coldness of it,
However lovely she will ever be;
But I pity you gods, that eternity precludes
Your hearts from death, for death is much of love,
And is why men can die content, having found
In one short life, all they desired to find.

[Daphne]

These things we know.

Vines being vines, and lovers being lovers,
We'll fancy lovers as vines and vines as lovers
Because they twine alike to life and glory;
Vines vine tho', for that is how they grow,
Blindly, naturally, wrapping in arms whatever's near, -
Whatever's there for them, given them, they take,
However the trellis fits their promise tomorrow;
And never, notwithstanding what hands may
Break them off or newly wind them, never may vines unvine
When new moods turn them against their plot
And make them regret their yesterday's passions;
Fickle, arrogant, undevout, thus love's vines vine, unvine, vine,
Restless not till love has run its seasons.

Once I laid seeds below a withered tree
And watched them weave the dead boughs
To make them live again, and could you show me
What young lover loves so purely I might believe
That love is birth and beauty, and not disease;
Earth's fragile lovers endure because they are not lovers
As we are; they take what will grow them, and merely grow,
Numb to what grows beside them, not pitying, never martyring
Themselves for weaker life, - so love's not selfless among flowers,
Nor selfish, being devoted, but perfect in the love of itself, undoubting
That love is best that always grows.

So let's not compare us;
Not lie love motivates flowers,
Knowing 'tis greed that is not greed
Because no flower doubts that life is greatest,
So together they all strive.

[Apollo]

Well I know the circling bowl will waft thy spirits to bliss.

Let vines, lovely, be vines, let lovers be lovers,
And let us say they're the same, -
You say there is a hint of us in flowers, but more divides us,
And you say we're not as lovely because our devotions change, -

Open your eyes, dove, and see the earth has many daughters;
You are one, and yet you dream that love is better in the forest,
As tho' you're not yourself a forest flower,
Able to love the same as any vine;

O flower, leave these thoughts that narrow you,
That hold you off the divine, and rather find
One loveliest flower, within yourself,
The vine;

You say that flowers grow;
You forget that they grow differently;
For some poison, some structure,
Some strangle, some shade others' growth;
No flower is as its forest, as no man
Is entirely as Men, but we may find one in one
And many in many without lowering our thoughts
To fancy.

You love flowers: be one then, and together with them
Brighten the earth for love;
          And know that love is forever
Because it is not how one but how everything grows.

[Admetos]

Oaths made for Love.

I.

They say that gods may love;
        I say
That they love not who may love forever;
Love lives not *for* itself *in* itself
But by its ending impending;
                Therefore,
        Let those who shall end
Love that which ends with them,
That in their end they may by love
Be comforted, and then in dying they forget
All of what love is and was.
              There is for Man
        But one vestige of mortal nature
Against the gods' dark region,
And that is love.

Below heaven, love is heaven's reflection, -
As above, so below, yet showing not so clearly,
But muddled with the earth and the unstable face,
Ever broken, ever changing, never the same.

And we are lovers, here below heaven,
And that is our strength.
It is not strong to live and not to love, -
Tho' love may seem weak, may seem frail,
Of all things nothing in *seeming* love excels;

For love is humanmost of all our passions, -
All for a better bliss we sacrifice a lesser,
Surrender a lonely self-absorption
For the twofold thrill of joys
And sorrows not our own.

II.

They say there was a maiden so lovely
She drew a god down from heaven,
The king of gods and men down from heaven
Made fall enamored, clothing the sun of his godliness
In a man's less blinding beauty, and night by night
Made love to her like a dream;

When the great god's wife discovered his indiscretion,
He turned the maiden to a heifer, told his wife
There was no maiden for him to love;
A false oath, made for love,
That a god desiring to know the joys
Of more fleeting human passion, swore because
There was no other way.

III.

And so God made love unbreakable,
And of all mortal things He only envies
Mortal love, and looks on earth from heaven
With weary acquiescent eyes, understanding
That heaven is not a place for love, having no endings
To make love dear;

And down He looks on the dark earth
And sees love last as long as love can last,
And men with short round lives knowing they cannot hold
Forever their dearest ones, nor hold what else is lovely
In themselves or in riverbanks or in meadows
Or in quiet seasons that melt and grow;
Men lack the eternal fairness of youth
That makes gods arrogant to love, tho' thus
Men know what gods are blind to: that everything lovely,
Tho' it may never sour in the eye, sours eventually
In the mind and the heart, and tho' gods' aspects
Stay with youth and never rupture, this holds them off
From what death grants, and that is an end to love,
And the rapturous passage of inexorable affairs;

The lover says *forever*, afraid of his oath,
Fearing to give all that he can give
To what may not for all of itself be so lovely
To the all-of-himself he has given to it, -
So youth fears giving youth to what may
Summer and autumn it, that oaths of a lifetime's love
Might kill life's spring, dousing the fires of fleeing desire
With bonds of confident devotion . . .
And so love's tempests cool to snow.

Love thus, tho', is not as love goes, -
Hours of love beat not love fuller in lovers' veins
If endless, and death frailing love makes life suffer
To make life strong, that love grows a part of life
And in spite of death, can never leave it;
And so, for love, all suffering twines into grace,
And if it must leave us, leaves but truly rests,
And again, as always, we embrace.

[Voice]

The Trees. If life be dear to thee, it must be dear to all.

I.

It is
The fruit before the root,
The furled fountainhead before
The full, blithe and fertile flowing, -
            True being,
Behind the lovely foreconception of the blossoming thought,
                Opens into life.

                So men fancy
        Flower over root.
So lovers embrace;
So lovers dream their love is free
From death, - their vanity is at once
Fully beautiful and fully absurd.
'Tis here they fail;
            No;
'Tis here they triumph over failure, -
For if success in living is not the acceptance
Of what seems natural, the most alive is then
The mind which can invent the finest
And the fairest reason for living;
We know that Man has never been content
To simply Be, and that is not Man's folly,
            No;
It is the deathless and unanswerable query
That never shall exhaust his yearning.

II.

O but tell us what is there in the sigh
And the rush and the whisper that alludes
To weariness and wisdom, as tho' we groan
Not under of the burden of numb boughs but
The weight of ancient life and deep deep prudence
That shakes its hoary mane upon the sight

Of seedling souls that waste the youth of their life
In withering distress? What is there in the forest
That does not rustle and sway and shimmer
That chance might make to seem like shrieks and murmurs,
Hums and moans and chatters and mutters and screams?
Fashion what you will of light winds' timbres and textures
As they play thorough the woodland's bending eaves,
But await no devotion to the urges and the oaths
And the notions they compel you to;
Think, if you will, that there are things in which
The forest believes, but never dream the trees
Will bind themselves to any enduring creeds.

III.

O tear-spilling man, what are you?
Did you weep so much for joy when you could hold
What now you've lost? Or is it death that breaks you
To materiality, shattering some lovely dream
You nursed in conscious ignorance
To keep your heart at liberty to love
And not to hoard? Or is the whole world mad
To watch its nigh brothers pass on without tears?

And will you weep for them, if you have more tears
Than for yourself is rain enough to cleanse
What sorrows sprung them? I deem you will,
As men are wont to, to find their grief strikes
Sympathetic strings in quiet birdsongs and mellow pastures,
And flowers that closing their heavy eyes softly
Will live to see the morrow; so everything
Harbors the sore heart, either vaguely
As some emblem of continuing life,
Or as some more intimate consolation
That seems to make the calmer elements
Yet standing by more love him; and they sing,
And they sing, the song of the human soul.

IV.

Bronze leaves lift in the warm dusk wind
And wail to the poppy skies, -
                    They whisper:

Beyond the sway and sigh of the voiceless bloom,
Beyond the long blue sky, the deep grey sea,
The tall dim moon, the towering stars;
Beyond the high bright shining sun, and the fancied voice
Of a summer's day and a summer's eve,
The one true voice within them all begins,
Twines among, and then their harmony resounds, -
And their song is the song of a thoughtless God
Perceived by a thoughtful soul.

But hush now, hush;
Take softly wind and sun, -
Till sun beaming warmly beget sleep,
And gentle winds exhale you to your slumber,
And fertile seas upon you rise and descend, -
And then life ends and life begins,
And out of death's voicelessness,
Perfect and serene,
New hearts resound.

[Daidalos]

Endymion.

Topaz eyes and hair of honey-blond,
And very beautiful youth, sinuous and dilating
And wandering youth, overgrown to a keen and doubting spirit
Dissatisfied with men's vain commotions diverting, void of sense,
With needless troubles, one's welling fount of life, to spill one's
Nimblest waters on the barren hungry beds
Between greed's flowerless shores, -

He told his heart, O Heart I will not fool you,
Not give you over to contracts with men
Who will but wring you out for what you're worth to them,
Squandering you to yourself; your true love knows
Your worth is greater, and loyal to no other,
Together we will find our truth.

So he said, and shook the guilty chains of obligation,
And leaving the city of his birth where men judged men
By all but faith to their souls, he became a wanderer,
Tending a little herd, drifting through forests and deserts
And tall cities above dark coasts, on paths bending the bare heads
And crooked backs of mountains and valleys,
And cliffs sheer-faced gazing beyond the sea
On dawns splitting the bronze waters;
And he passed dark thundering ocean-spilling nights
Caving himself below whatever bough or ledge could offer a gabling hand,
Till the loud sprawling heaven of clouds widened into silence,
And showed through massive panes of misty glass the calm stars
And the dove-whiteness of their mist-shawled queen,
The moon.

And at length, finding all cities the same, all men the same,
All hopes the same, all passions the same, and knowing at last
That men had nothing he desired, he parted from them,
And drove his small white flock into the wilderness
Along the rugged slopes of the immaculate unpeopled coast
Following no paths, intending no end to his journey,
And sought the promised bliss of the only splendid star

That none could seek before him, or bring him having traced, as all he
        desired
Was an honest portion of the earth, not sullied with the noise
Of amusing and comforting and stifling and feeble and absurd lies,
But so fully honest to itself that he need never fear his own dishonesty;

And so as no man can but find his own share of heaven,
He sought the virgin pastures over which his heart's star hung,
And on an evening of violent upheaval darkening
Heaven and earth, appealing to the hills for shelter,
At last he discovered what he sought.

[Endymion]

On the humanity of solitude.

I.

O you lovers of nights of calm stars,
Of lush full amaranth twilights
Like lovers bleeding their violet love
In rivers down the orb of the sky . . .

O you shy lovers of the shy pure moon
Whose passions dance on star-crowned hills
Like evening stars aloft at the golden hour,
Bearing the slumbrous world to bowers of deep
And peaceful dreams, and the small pains and toils
Of their worlds are forgotten . . .

O you small swift bird, flying silently there
Across the stars! You are more shadowed than they are
And so your silhouette stands forward in silent motion . . .
So high above the night-shaded clusters of the trees
I see your dark wings wading yon deep-toned
Deepest-of-all-seas . . . Why fly you so softly
And without a word? and let your wingsong fade, ah!
With its own creation . . .

It has rained, but with the going of the sun
The rain has gone, and the clouds have drawn
Their veil away and the night is tinkling
With the afterfall of rain on leaf, on
Lower leaf, on leaf lower, leaf lowest, and lost;
This dark instrument sprays against the sky
More deeply dark than the deep far sky
That breaks with the light of the stars . . .
And there is a music if you listen, for when
A thousand leaves are played upon all rhythms
Merge, mingle, come together, -
And all, all in the world is rhythm;
Pitch is only color.

I stand beneath these rain-soaked boughs and lift my face
To what comes falling . . . Round me everywhere
I hear the soft notes play, and feel the ones that coldly strike,
And feel I am not hearing the melody of another,
But building with this other a song that is the sound on us
Of what naturally falls.

II.

O how, if in star-solitude and deep-sea-loneliness
We somehow find within ourselves God's voice
Singing wisdom to the soul; if both song and silence
Of natural and numinous bequeath both rhythm and melody
To the lyrical temperament of the heart which yearns
For no bare pulsation nor unvaried monotone nor deep grave note sustained,
But love song and serenade, lilt, lay, hymn and carol,
Glee for all beginnings - lively, brisk - psalm for the heart of day - vigorously
        rising -
Lullaby to the light's last hour - love's diminishment -
On into the night, tho' in the end no requiem,
But roundelay life's variations - majestically softening - and perishing,
Run out like rain the epigram beauty of a life's refrain . . .

O how, if thus we gain our truth, thus our contentment,
Can the company of other men, to a heart that does not need
Their faithless envies and thin desires, be more than a disease
To the duty of intimate honesty
That compassion compels him to sacrifice,
Guilt in the guise of pity folding him shamelessly
Against himself, so that he wastes his independent soul
On flaws he knows he cannot mend, being others'?

To be humane is not to try to keep everything alive,
But to live yourself, and to be uniquely human
In the most honest way.

[Voice]

The Streambed. Passing the bounds of life assigned by fate.

I.

Some may dream, and may the dream believe,
That love may live beyond death;
That for a living moment love may live on
Single and unattached, until the love
By fully dying becomes inviolate, pure, and undivided,
Death unbreaking what life and death mingled
First broke;

      So broken, this dream,
These accidents interweaving, these echoes coupling,
Trilling, purling, braiding moments in an endless flow;
A man there, on the bank, looks for himself
In the lapping rill, and sees, only, his face,
Sees not that this freshet more nearly reflects
His soul, which always is coupling, always interweaving,
Always trilled, braided and purled by the fluent
And refluent world whose echoes strike always
That part of him which less resembles stones and clay
Than streams and rain;

      Rain down on them you lovely world,
And make rivers flow down from their mountains
To their valleys, blooming the tender seeds that lie
Buried there within them; you must tell men once more
How came to them their love to compare themselves
To fields and mountains, and all that is grand
And beautiful, for too often they forget that their spirit
Rests not only in how the world *is*, but also in how men *view*
What wraps them; O so often men overlook
The depths of feeling, blinded by the fronts,
The surfaces of things; so the lake, ocean or stream
Will seem as bodies, moving as one, as tho' solid,
As tho' together;

Togetherness tho'
Is unreactive, unmoving, passive, and therefore dwells nowhere
In this world of changes;

Changing always, always interlacing,
Twining, tangling, penetrating, - so men weave with the world;
And as the movements beyond measure of waters
Are dilated in Man's eye to a golden ribbon
Unfolding to the sunrise, so is he that dilation
Whereby unnumbered purposeless motions,
Commingling beneath the ostensible changelessness
Of a man's appearance, bequeath to the creativity
Of his perception the golden dream
Of Permanence;

Permanent, he deems, and lovely forever,
His loveliest dreams; his loves he would have last
To the end of time;

O Time, Man's confusion,
Flowing as rivers flow: you have whispered
A million million times in men's ears that nothings lasts;
They have heard you, and yet refused to believe;
Forgive them tho', - the deepness of their feelings
Overwhelms them, and when moments gather
Which are beautiful to them, which seem to hint
That love makes eternities of beloved hours and souls,
Then they dream the human dream,
That love may live on.

II.

Onward, you drops of tears and rain,
Flow onward . . .
Not long these voices last,
Nor will rain from dark clouds fall forever;
The sun will rise on days as glorious as men can dream of,
And lively colors yet will spread out calmly over the sky
After the storm and flood and joyless banks have drawn away;
The sun will flare and glisten on trees and emerald meadows,
And roses become rubies, and bluebells become sapphires,

And this massive light shining suddenly
Redeems the rain-drooped world
On which it shines;

      Shine on, then,
And show men what they are,
For as water flashing in the sun
They are for a moment the glory they reflect,
And tho' a rose is, only, a rose, and a meadow is, only, a meadow,
And they are the same before and after the rain
Has fallen upon them, their loveliness magnifies
As they take life again from the rains that bowed them down,
And mist off their purified faces to the sun's benevolence,
Who loved them before the clouds, and now loves them again
When the clouds have parted;

      And when these billows part
Will men be parted from their sorrows;
Too frail to believe they will fully die,
Hour's flowers, as they are, for but a glance
Of heaven's gleaming ring, live whole lives
In the impermanent affections of a god
And giver of life, who by so giving
Falsely by men is fancied to love and to eternally tend
Those things he births and blooms; for in truth,
After the blossom, there is but the god-ordained death
And the falling away;

      And the falling away
Is not a perishing, but a birth that blends
And levels the accumulations they are
Out of the imbalances they've made themselves
To the firm foundations wherefrom
The raw coherent world
Rationally rises, -

      And rising out of sorrow
To a blended indifference, they'll find fruition
Beyond the last breath, content in parity,
And they'll then, lone tumbling raindrops,
Fountain and river, ride to the sea.

III.

As on sea or river
Skies drift and shores gleam,
So now daffodils glow on the margin,
And golden-yellow beside their brink the waters flow,
And into their curled colors he pours tears from two
That are the very same face to his mind:
The face that cries, and the face they show;

      But tho' his face may rest
On the surface of these waters, and countenance,
In the clear shallows shimmeringly,
The golden bed of this stream so full of light,
He looks not deeply enough if there, he thinks,
He finds his soul;

His soul is, rather,
The water itself, flowing.

[Daidalos]

Till age crept slowly on.

I knew from feathers on the waves that he had fallen,
Thence been shattered by the soft-hard sea,
And circling high above the surf,
Long I sought the body of my boy, -
   Sought and sought through night and day
     The body of my boy -
But saw I not again his beloved face -
    'Twas not, it seems, the will of the shore;
The sea lay flat and showed my shadow back to me
      Unpityingly;
For all my tears the sea lay calm and would not lift him free;
Yet bode I there below the cliff-dark shore
   And waited, -
     For what, I cannot say.
I think perhaps I could not bear to leave
The spot of sea which held my young Adored;
    Could not bear
The unanswering sea, the silent sea, the solemn face
That met my prayers and pleas with naught
But murky waters, roll on roll.

O God! O Heaven! O Blessed Beyond!
O soul sailing free to lands of perfect loveliness!
O how I wish I could believe, as one who never doubts, in so innocent a
  dream!
O how sweet it must be to absolutely have a soul!
   How sweet to know
That life is not impermanent configuration,
Not merely one mere moment's frail interplay
Of failing flesh, frame, and limited brain,
Nor which formation going once is gone forever,
But is immortal substance borne out of and dying into
An endless and yet knowable stream.

They say that love transcends the hollow form;
O heart be strong in this, I tell you, I tell you once more,
That love is abiding, that love is not a season, but forevermore;

And yet in spite of all I say to my own self
To soften my own misery, still yearns
Some insatiable fragment of my love for him
That I bore undreaming I would have to endure my life
Without his love returned;
              Indeed I feel
That but to see once more his hazel eyes,
                    Tho' lifeless, -
To see him out of vagueness risen, and as himself
To float between the pearl-grey sky and sea, -
To once more see him as I knew him once to be, -
'Tis this great hope that keeps at bay
The pendulous song of the shore,
        Song against the life
I hope may come for him and me,
          Against the dream
That altho' the heart must die, the soul is free.
And so I wait beside the sea.

[Voice]

The Wind. Not to do this would be the greatest wrong.

Lover, drift on.

I bring you lavender from fields afar, -
Take this gift before it goes
And slips your desperate hands;
O fool in love,
The things you love will kiss your heart and sail away;
The seasons pass, and draw along their scents and splendors,
Like runs of melody our memory preserves, -
Preserving them as only something lovely to us,
But their tones' precise array
Our wistfulness cannot revive.

You kneel among daffodils because a winter has come
And withered your field's fairest flower, -
You came to rain your tears on springtime yellow
And springtime savor, that Death's gloom within you
Might drown in Life's suffusing color,
And Life's genial swirls of fragrant breath,
And you are not wrong to search for healing
Among these yellow blooms.

But know that you will never find her again
Exactly as she was, and as you loved her,
Nor would you ever have, had she never gone away;
The dream she was for you beautifies in the wake of her passing,
Not because you embellish more to what she was,
But because we true lovers never learn to love
What rolls tenderly through us, until that tender wind
Has drawn away.

Reach out, dear man, and call her name, -
I will bear your grief and blend your somber hymns
With hills' and seas' and valleys' aromas;
See that one gust goes, bearing one more cry away,
And now another flows over and through, and who can say
What lovely scents this new wind carries on

And carries away?

Seek, therefore, seek what you loved in her
In every breeze, - whatever fragments of beauty in the world
Came together to make her so lovely,
Have lately spread themselves and lost themselves
In the world again, and if you would have her
Once more in your embrace, you must now learn
To draw them for a second time
Together in your heart.

You are what the wind is, and nothing is a part of you forever;
Once, for a time, as you gazed lovingly on daffodils,
Lavender came on the wind and enfolded you,
And the wind sighed, saying, Love what blooms before you,
And never trust the wind that brings you lovely things
You cannot hold.

You will leave these blossoms, dear man,
Or they will die and leave you, - they will not
Stay to be the solace of your soul, and if you wait
They will come round again, but never will be the same;
You will wait for what came once on the wind, was there for a moment,
And then was borne away, and you cannot live on the hope
That fair winds once more will collide and carry you back
To the moments you loved.

Roam, lover, with fragrant memories in your open heart
Over the hills and the valleys and the seas
And gather them to you and carry them, -
Until who you are and what you seek, converge;
And then, dear man, you and she are reunited.

And so, dear lover,
Drift on.

[Apollo]

From eyes that never weep.

Once again with a golden sigh
The day has failed to ride forever,
And into the dusk of another companion
The light is fading and fading and fading . . .

What is there to hold up life that must be
Upheld forever? Is this madness, what we are?
Flesh, and yet not flesh, as frail as men are,
And yet without death to cure our desirousness;

Perhaps the fleetingness of desire
Is why one must die at last
To make devotion bearable;
Or perhaps desire flees
When passion's fire from a soul
To whom everlastingness can mean
The only devotion, frightens the beloved
With thoughts of how it is too endless
To be possible;

O how I wish the sweet savor of a green crown
Could sink my soul into dreams of you . . .
Sovenaunce of a sailed sweetness;

For even to wake alone again
Would never be
A renewal of grief.

[Voice]

The Mockingbird. She wishes to behold the radiance of the sun.

Sometimes - life - is too brief -
Love - is too fleeting - life is
Dying - ever - dying - ever -
Living - never too - alive - never fully
Loving - always fearing - love in vain -
Not brave enough - to fully live - nor strong enough -
To freely love - unafraid of - death's abandonment;
Not blithe enough - to sing allthrough the seasons -
Nor blithe enough to sing while loving one girl only
Songs not just for one.

Freedom - there is - freedom - in dying - and the dead are
Freer - freer - freer - freer - free;
Free her - let her - flow away - hold her -
No longer - nor try reclaiming - what has fled -
Not your's - life's - love -
Nor try to hold too close
What has to leave.

Surrender her - death has - ended her - has -
Mended her - by - ending her; - nor death nor she will ever hear
Your plea, plea, plea.

You loved a girl - and now that girl -
Is star-far-away;
                      She was - and is now -
In memory - as she was - and will remain - in memory -
As you loved her, -
                      Weep, weep, weep no longer;
Sing instead the life she graced.

Deep, deep, deep - your love is - deep -
Your love is - what makes you deep;
Life's beauty - O lover - lies less - in loving -
Lies more - in taking leave; - for love is -
Fairmost - because you love - what flees;
Why love? - for this: of what is human,

Only love seems eternal.

Remember her - but let her - sleep - let her -
Sleep - release her - she must - *must* - leave.

Keep alive - her love given - let go - what love she could not give;
Let love last - let hope - out of memory - live on - her soul -
Live on;
          The girl goes - must - go - you stay;
Until you follow.

Life is not, good soul, gone to you, -
Heaven - her heaven - your heaven - only at life's natural end
Is consummated;
                'Tis misery - and grief in vain -
That sunders all forever.

                    Live then - strong in the strength
Of her love while it lasted, till closes this life of expectation
Upon your joyful hopeful heart and heaven spills like a fountain
Dry from youth and youth imbues to that frail wisp of you
That youth abandoned, and a thousand thousand memories
Draw round you, dance, and are yours again, and heaven opens like loves
        regained
In one last loveliest dream, and all of life's losses roll away, she rises,
And is yours once again.

III

SURRENDER

CLARIFICATION *of* CONTEXT

ADMETOS, wandering, as night comes over the world; he dwells on the parting; Daidalos pondering the death of his son; his vacillations between sympathy and anger; how he nearly abandons hope;

Hylas, wandering in search of a spring, discovers a lovely forest pool; how the nymphs of those waters, enamored of his beauty, swiftly draw him down to their palace far below; he cries out; his cries heard by one who relays the strange incident to Heracles; how Heracles, distraught, dashes off from the Argonauts on the shore to seek Hylas in the forest;

Endymion ponders the night; his meditations on the true nature of individuality; dreaming, he is overcome by the ardor of a woman, her soft beams kiss him, she lies at his side; waking, he finds his loneliness unbearable; emerging to the night, he finds the low crescent moon familiar, like a lover; he reaches out in desperation, he pleads with her to return;

Heracles, weary after days of fruitless searching, sleeps on the bank of a forest pool; dreams of Hylas rising in shadow; how the shadow bids Heracles leave him to his life below; his farewell, and he sinks away; how, waking, the great man reaches out to catch his fading child, but catches nothing; how he dives into the fountain to retrieve him, yet finds only empty depths;

Reluctantly, having waited long for their companions to return, and unable to spurn any longer the favorable winds, the Argonauts loose the cables of the Argo, and depart; despondent, they fly across the sea, deeply saddened by the abandonment of their friends; deep in the night, Orpheus sings prophecies in the darkness, illuminating the loss of Hylas and Heracles; how the sea-god Glaucos sang these truths to his ears; and how the men of the Argo feel calmer in their hearts for obtaining this closure;

Heracles, defeated, returns at last to the shore, only to find that the others have gone; lastly, how he finds the body of Icaros, and buries him in a cave above the sands.

[Admetos]

Though the gifts of youth are mine.

I. Hope, as it is.

Love disintegrates, love comes apart, love
Comes to pieces;
                        O yes in the beginning
There are the happy years, the first and loveliest years,
The virgin, pure, faultless, flawless, perfect years;
                        O yes there is the birth,
The birth of Beauty, the birth of Love, birth
Of Love's hierarchy, Love's division, Love's
Selection, condemnation, judgment of this world's range
Of Graces, of Lovelies, and of Fairs.
                        O yes there is the dalliance, the desire,
The long for, lust for, burn for, the pursuit,
The tenderness and the devotion, the slow devotion;
And then the fall not a falling, the madness
Of love in variance, of loved not loving, and loving
Tho' not loved the same. And for some fortunate few
There is the joy of some loves realized at last.

Often I have wondered
How to live, love and suffer,
If I am I but one short life and then dust forever;
                        For is not Forever
                The hope that makes bearable
The passing of a moment's loveliness?

We are not through yet, she said,
Our love is yet alive . . . Live no less
Fully now, my love, she said,
You loved me, yes, I know you loved me;
If you love me still, let me go . . .
I would not have you love me
If I cannot love you in return . . .

Ah, sweetness! . . . How strong she was
To weep only a tear a two, to utter a few more

Lovely half-sentiments, to hold me in those
Deeply trembling eyes, kiss me once,
And quietly die;

All at once, I am broken;
The mind seeks benevolence,
Fumbles for a haven, a respite, a release:

Aloofly stand the shy shadows
Whose distal being reawakens
Unapproachably severed;
Of what souls in life they were a share
They yet live on in, are not unalterably
Lain to rest, nor are lost, nor are
Suppressed, not to be forgotten
Before the flood of riper experience,
But to pattern upon unsentimental Nature
        An order accepting
Of Beauty's brief dissolving day.

Therefrom in each man wells
The fountain of his memories, outpouring to his sight
His own reflection, faultless as his life;
And in the evocation of his past he generates
The hopes which are his heavens,
Wherein the loves of his life not only
Shall re-appear, but in his embrace indissolubly shall remain,
Not vaguely as Love lived, but lucidly as Love completely dear,
And therefore not Love itself,
But Love's Idea.

So comforts the mind;
But stronger now, the homily of the heart:

The things that were
Console the things that are;
Love is a dream, an ever-flowing stream,
A fragrant arbor, a flowered dell,
Amid a forest ever green;

Love, lost and gone -
Gone - unreachable -
Lost - nor ever shall be found -
Here, living, with me, living,
Never again, no,
Never again,
Fled, fled, fled forever, -
Gone where? Somewhere;
Somewhere beneath blue valleys,
Or in blue air above the clouds, -
Far past day and night, on temperate slopes,
Untouched from what I knew you last to be;

Sweetly-dreaming, it could be, under boughs
Of a balmy oak-swell, islet of sun-luster loose
In the swale and swell of auburn prairielands'
Endless dusk, I know not;

The hope is this:
I do not doubt that on the day I die,
Before these eyes close wearily upon
This bright vision that is life, I shall see
Waiting in the open doorway, like the brightest memory
Of younger days, the fair bride
I once wed, and loved,
And lost too early.

Beyond her shall be the fields, the trees, the waters,
The distant mountains and the sunlight upon them;
And I shall take her by the hand, and led by her
I shall not fear the going away, not fear
The fading of this life, knowing that only
Beyond this fragile dream may death
Never part us again; and I shall leave
Not sadly, but forgetting as I go
The loneliness and the desolation and the
Heart much-broken, and the hateful darkness
That carried her away; and she
Will walk before me, walk with me,
Like a dream, like a memory will lead me far away,
In the end as in the beginning, for the end

Is heaven, and heaven was born in the beginning,
When love was born in the faraway beginning,
In the so dim glad beginning, so dim,
But the end is clear, and she shall lead me round
To this time again, this moment, this youth again,
And all shall be again as when we parted,
Nor shall pain be, nor partings, but shall be
As all things are far away, where all is forever
As we could never hold in life for more
Than a fading day, not love as lived in one
Or a lifetime of days, but as, my dear, I hear her say,
You leave one mortal bed for one in which
Pure love can finally lay.

Such is hope;
Leaves us answerless
In a dusk our own;
We say: There can be!
Say: There cannot be . . .
            Life again as we have lived it.

So along the shadow now
Stars and vapors sweep, and hymn
That not for love should lovers weep;
Love is a haven, wherein the solaced heart
May rest from grief, and drowse
Within remembered oaths and prayers;
And from the silence of a finished soul
Will know what heaven was and may be,
And in the strength of this, may strongly
Beat, beat, beat,

Once more, finally, and forever, my love,
In heaven we shall meet.

II. Hope, what it falls to.

Insipid lies! Trite dead lifeless heaven!
You think I desire you? A flicker of a weakness,
Flutter of a hunger, broken-hearted thoughts
That halt at how I'd hold her

If I found her once again alive;
But there they root themselves,
And will not imagine on to what two souls would say
When joined again beyond death;
To dream the bliss their love made of life
Could ever be strong enough to make life live again,
Is to forget the vital bond of natural love
To natural life;

Bear in mind the folly of blind devotion,
The folly of giving too much to anything,
Of making of death a pleasant sky-voyage
Over the river of the sea to a blissdom
Lovelier than life, yet not so far from what we knew
So as to reave us of what kept us
Upon the former shore;

I've learned so much about love
In loving one girl only, how we desire most
What we leave behind; I cannot misremember you,
Unlearn you, efface you from the reveries
That bring me back to the beginning, reviving to pain
Our early bliss that would be best forgotten
Could I choose to make them dim and myself
Less haunted by so many heavens I never knew I had
But now have certainly lost; not only lost, but hopelessly lost,
Unable to recall, unable to forget; but not for anything would I will
One lone less thought to settle pensively through me
And allow Unforgettable She to sink away
A little more destroyed, a little more utterly lost;

Go then, I told her within myself,
Be a bright moment, not a full life's joy,
And tho' I would still love you amid the rain,
Off I drift now into the sea of you, where still reflects
The sky of our love, and the sun and the stars of our love,
And the moon and the birds and the clouds of our love,
And even the face that loved you, that must now look
On only what was lovelier in your eyes, therein to find
The soul of the one who gazed on this
And found this worthy to love;

We dream that two may two remain forever;
Not so, perhaps;
        There is:
The breath that falters, the young love
            Early ended;
Withdrawn the interacting tones that sang
(As of myself I go on singing)
The song of another self,
And we, tho' two,
As one did sing.

It is a fair resignation, she told me, to know
That two may sing a twining song no longer,
Only one, one, one heart may course on with the blood of two,
And the heart beating on may be his or yours,
His by your blood, yours by his,
And knowing this to reason:
I die, and he lives, - gladly then, I die.

The far-off death-moment, that should be fearless,
Should be culmination, climax, reunion,
If we truly believe those hopes that eased
Our severest losses;

For on that day
We are as lovers in the dawn light.
                Fall
The tears of blended joy and pain, the melancholy gloom
Of former delights all at once recollected, the strong embrace
Of all we love and cannot bear to lose.
                And then the final kiss,
        A broken word or two,
And then two paths in the dew.

To all fair things we knew we sing, in death,
        Our last aubade.

[Endymion]

Night. Aloofly he stands.

I have no god but the evening,
                No love
But the indigo evening, the clear dark night, the sheer high stars,
                Through to the dawn, cerise.

            I am alone,
And in my loneliness have found myself my equal.
                Heaven may say
That here is a man who is his own,
Who has in himself no trace of any other,
And that is how I wish to be.

Still - the world is - still.
Still, so very still, the silver hills,
Silent upon them the starry midnight glint.
What fair shadows their long rolling backs describe,
When dark grass bedewed by the soft cold evening
Glows and gleams with the light of the pallid moon!
O how I love these silent heights and valleys
When tented by the silent distant stars!
My praise to you good God whose heaven lies here serenely quiet
Among the slanted half-lights and deep full darks,
And blue-black skies spinning with fires faint and faraway . . .

            O bliss!
Apart from all shoal courtesies, all meaningless consociation,
All vain self-worshipping overproud solipsism,
I range on long dim grasslands,
                But by the moment lead
            Along a random way.

The sunless unilluminated world
Flows riverine through my soul, day's end ending
The din and clamor of the agitated
Tumultuous globe; O tell me what troublous brain
Finds peace among the garish decorations
Of those dense teeming cities that glow so starkly

Even in the deepest depths of tranquil night?

        O fairmost fall!
Dusk lays to bed the fallen sun beneath the claret west,
And all tall things their low deep sable selves lengthen,
Lengthening void to void, darkness closing all,
Blending color out of shade.

Deepen strangely, fields into oceans,
Mountains mantle into vast waves, -
O what is in mountains that is so comforting
When on clear nights they rest beneath the stars
Their vast blue shadows, behind them the yet distant dawn's
Dim glowing, seeming to hold their massive bulks
In gesture of embrace? . . . And O the shadow-laden hills
And whatsoever may slumber on them, slumber under them,
And valleys full of silver light wherein is dreamt
The darkest and the lightest dreams, is dreamt
By all that slumbers beneath these hills of grass
That lay serene like some great sea, its massive waves
Suspended or slowly rolling, death's dark dream . . .

Before this evening love-mothering Beauty
Never fairer dreamed in dew-impearled meadow,
Nor raven-velvet ridge, moonstruck stream;
Nor dwelt upon soul has ever
A lovelier queen; queen temperate, just, fair,
Beautiful to gaze upon, - changing ever,
And yet ever the same.

I watch her sail among the leaves,
Now seen clearly, now a hidden glow, -
The night is clear, with not a cloud to veil her,
And as she sails above the trees, I walk below;

There bends the frail thin anabranch, commingling with leaves, -
There the tall ridge looms above the upland trees benighted, -

A star falls from the sky, -
        Out of the darkness
One single star descends and dies in a half-seen stream of light, -

A moment goes, and the sky is cold, still, distant, full as ever, -
            To my wide all-embracing eyes
No star, no light, no loveliness has left yon lustrous round
Spreading above me;
                        I wait,
Trying to watch the stars move on.
But they stream too slowly, too vast a voyage make
Along their vast hidden circuits, and I cannot follow,
Cannot slow myself to their vastly different tempo,
Their unfathomably slow arching, slow as all
Everlasting things must be, -
            Indeed,
We know our limitations because this one sky
Overwhelms us, and we can only barely see
The swiftly-falling stars.

I am a wanderer,
And if aimlessness is drifting like the moon,
Then we two shall sway together,
Pursuing our vain desires.

[Daidalos]

Of dreams.

I long lay pondering;
            Saw I
The four walls high around me, the two small eyes
Upon me, eyes of a little son gazing on his father, -
                  Hope is in that gaze,
            And a love so sincere,
And in his love knew he his father would not stand by
And allow these walls to hold his burgeoning life;
                  He knew,
      That even the highest prison
Could not stifle him and me;
                        'Twas in his eyes I saw this -
            The eyes full of love
And not of tears, that seemed to say,
Come what may, we two shall be together,
            Shall take our life together,
Whether in the dank or in the open air we still shall live
                        Together, come what may.
And so pondering long I lay; I looked,
And saw the sky our only way.

Not dreamless do we rest;
Our fantasies without in the long hereafter,
            Our life is lost in slumber.
The senseless dead in earthy darkness drowse,
Buried souls not souls beyond death's quietus,
Eclipsed by their own final incarnation.
                  We live
            But to give our fancy flight.

We aspire
But to the height of our own visions,
            Nor may we pass them;
Ourselves we may but shallowly fathom
In daylight displays of wit,
But the puremost mind is locked away,
Enwrapped within its images, -

Blemished, upon awakening, for then we stand
Beyond the pour of free imagination;
                    And when, by daybreak,
              Our nightlong visions melt away,
We find our hands not able
To limn beautifully enough the sea within us,
The thoughts and emotions and all that rests
Deep and dark and beyond our knowing;
All that yearns by being fair to us, and beautiful,
                            Yearns to be raised,
Compelling to articulation, to illustration,
The beauties seen firstly by the soul, felt by the heart,
And then for others conveyed
By the head and hand.

And yet we linger;
Eyes open in the shadow of a dream's passing
We lie hunting in the darkness of dead visions
For something clear and comprehensible, -
O wild fantasies! Irrepressible, unsolvable, overpowering,
Abandoning us to the rush and whirl and violence of the world
As it truly collides with us;
              And so we linger
In the afterglow of our own true being,
And doubt, for a blurred moment,
That anything is truly real;
And we wonder:
                    Can truth come softly in the night?
         Ah, but *softly?*
                        Indeed, the night is soft,
                 The stars and moon move softly,
              And the dimday world is softened
           From the frenzy of the blue vibrant day;
But not softly do our dreams convey us
From the firmer world, rather in a passionate frenzy
That supples the strong unbending columns
On which all things stand, and the world
Becomes malleable, and we ourselves become malleable,
And for both ourselves and the world *impressions,*
And the feelings they inspire,
Govern all experience.

Thus we dream, and from these wanderings
In realms our own we come to know, from the
Colors we cause and the world causes in us we find
What life is, and the calming truth that nothing is behind life
That gives order to life and meaning to life,
And the consolation that only life
Gives life significance;

The inexhaustible flow of sensations
Flows on over us, and on and on,
And we cannot stifle what purely enters us
From flowing out again and overflowing from us;
Else the current we oppose will sweep us tumbling away,
And the rainbowed splendors of Time's onward growing, -
Seed-burstings and morning-gloryings and noonday sunflowerings,
And pale moonflowerings and star-shaped shadings of the night, -
Which might have filtered through us
To become by touching us beautifully human,
Flow on, unilluminated, into the dark sea
Wherefrom glimmers formlessly
The heralding wraith who whispers ominously
That soon we die and all is not yet ours.

   O deep yearnings!
O yearnings deep as tall! O desperate burning indistinct desire!
We worship you not enough, you half of us! You cradle of us
While we sleep, well of us, heavens of us, you wide mysterious sea of us;

Life you are, and the burden of life;
    At once our essence, our soul,
      You are as well the gate
        That locks the soul away.
There is too much in life; too many things will come to us, and go,
And their loveliness was ours for but the hour they were there;
      O life, and love too swift!
Too much of what we see we cannot know,
Too much of our experience is pure sensation,
Too much of life shall swiftly pass, passing like
A half-remembered dream.

[Glaucos]

His youth to all gave pleasure.

He was a youth of ethereal fairness,
Of a comeliness not varied,
Not subject to various translation,
But fair to all.

Three nymphs dancing in the falling sun, so fair,
Light fight prancing, bodies soft and young.

That a man may glint in immortal eyes,
Declining their apathy - unsympathetic -
To a blemished passion, thenceforth harboring a love
Not sprawling and general, but exclusive, singular and confined,
Yoking themselves to the whim of transient Sense . . .
So dissolve all dreams of eternity spent
In summer pools.

And he came to their glade in a golden haze,
Purple-shouldered, eyebright and trailing light,
An auraed, beautiful sight,
Admired by hidden eyes.

For beneath the water's hazy veneer
The enraptured goddesses peer with euphoric regard, -
His voluptuous beauty each heart entwines
And jealousy ruptures from fear.

He kneels at the brink of their crystalline spring
And lowers a palm to cull its trembling clarity;
He finds the fountain fresh, sweet, cold and lovely,
And dips now down the pitcher of bronze,
Gathering the waters' cold transparency.

They rise through lilies . . .
Golden heads lifting out of vagueness
Into the splintered light of the afternoon sun;
Like lucid gems the water earthward beads,
Winding down diminishing through woven tresses,

Along crescent brows and vibrant orbs
Of marvelous resplendence,
Past flushing lips and satin ridges
Of exquisitely dewy youth,
Down the concave hollows of ivory arcs
To glisten on naked shoulders,
Thence below to vanish in the drifting folds
Of sapphiric radiance,
Pellucid gowns shifting, light as wind,
Loosely robing the supple bends
Of magnolia skin.

Around his kneeling form the goddesses
Lift and glide, aloft in the splendor
Of mystical luminosity, bird-like,
Now fall feathering . . .

And swiftly they draw him
With barely a ripple, draw him,
Wonder-paralyzed, into their haven
Far below the loud-winded world . . .
Barely a moment goes, and everything
Is silent; the sun falls away; glow
Of an amber west swirled through
With swarthiness of smoky clouds.
The stars on smooth water rest.

A wanderer, had he heard his drowning cries,
Might with lifted eyes have sifted skies
For a loon to light on . . . a loon, or whatever mortal spirit can
So wildly dwindle, full of the melancholy of fate,
Into the laughter of its own tremolo.

[Daidalos]

Demophon.

Demeter, goddess of the earth, wandering,
Searching for her stolen daughter, in human guise
Lodged with Celeos and Metaneira, taking their child,
Demophon, over to nurse, and desiring
To give him immortality, began, night by night,
To purify his flesh with flames.

And day by day the child grew godlier,
And shed away his mortal smallness
To grow at a diviner pace.

But as the boy so grew,
His parents looked on, confounded.
His mother, suspecting something foul of the nurse,
One night concealed herself, and saw her Demophon
Offered to the glowing blaze.

She leaped out with a cry
And lifted her Demophon safely away,
Burning her hands.

The goddess, in fury, revealed herself by radiating
With a more than mortal brightness,
And Metaneira fell away in terror,
Cradling her son.

Said the goddess, Dumb mother,
You who are your child's burden,
Child who must battle, or take on, your stupidities,
Have now cut short a ritual beyond your understanding,
Saving your Demophon from a larger life,
To live a trifling one instead.
By fire was I making him a god,
By fire purifying, distilling, rarefying
His elements to their godliest essentials;
And yet what hope have the eternal and the wise
Of making gods of those beneath the care of vacant guardians,

Who preclude their charges from the enjoyment of so many joys,
Because they seem, to their judgment, like perils?
Let your fire-withered hands be your reward,
For for your Demophon assuring a narrow life,
When he may have been sacred, beautiful,
And broad.

So saying, the goddess vanished on a golden cloud,
And left the shrunken Demophon in the
Blackened hands of Metaneira, who wept
In the shadows of the flames.

[Hylas, Heracles]

Sacred. Beautiful. Broad.

I. Potential and Dissipation

If I am beautiful,
And if there is something in my gaze
That stirs hearts to lovely hopings,
And if the agreements of pleasant harmony
Pronounce in my appearance the virtues
Of charm and rare loveliness, I cannot claim these powers
As a part of my soul. Whatsoever I have of beauty's blush
Acts freely, powerful not as I will it to be,
But as others are sensitive to its power.

What are these blessings we are born with?
And what part of perfection is in those things
We have and cannot change? Sometimes too much
I find myself tempted to delight in other fair flesh
That craves me, seeing me fair and assuming our hearts
Are the same; but I have seen these lustful women
Who hide behind fair faces and lovely eyes
The urges and the vanities that make them hollow
And less than human, and I have seen how their beauty lasts
For a furious moment, then darkens when we find them useful
Only for pleasure, adequate only for the circling of appetites and satiations
And hopeless for the soul's higher reachings for truths and meanings,
And deeper gentler calmer modes of feeling;

But that is how beauty devours itself, and ruins itself,
Too intent on the selfish enjoyment of itself, never considering
That beauty may be a burden, and a promise to other men
Of Man's potential, - and thus
There is little a man can do
That is more pathetic and more unsightly
Than to squander what in him is lovely to others
On the decaying idleness of unquenchable lust.

II. Ideal and Expectation

The child is born beautiful;
Shall we love him for it?
Or will envy boil our blood to wrath?
As tho' he took what others must labor for;
As tho' he enjoys the rights of sublimity not his own;
Thus many would seek to vilify his birthright;
They fail to see how many ideals
His beauty compels him to live up to,
How the fairnesses born with him are not privileges,
But callings to something higher than what is painless and common,
And he bears them heavily, knowing that much is desired.

So the boy is born beautiful;
What is made easy for him?
That his beauty draws beauty?
But beauty draws admiration as well;
And what is admiration but expectation?
What do others expect but wonders to come
From so beautiful a being? And ugliness is nothing
But that which brings forth what is less than itself;
Woe, then, to the beautiful man, for so many things are less than he is!
O how much the gods demand of the virtues they give to us,
And how much we men demand of other men
To whom the gods have amply given;
We call the Beautiful *blessed,* and that they are,
But we bless only that which we revere, and demand the most from;
For what would beauty be if we called beautiful
Only what was easiest and least strivable?
And our jealousy should never be that others possess
The beauties we desire, but that they wither their beauty
On luxury and beauty's display.

III. Fairness and Proportion

The ungifted, the trodden-on say, Nothing in this world is fair!
We then must make the world fair; and we shall declare
Our struggle greatest who must create beauty
For ourselves;

Ah, but no god has built fairness
Into the order of things, and you who must
Struggle to fashion beauty from your ugliness
Are not greater than those who must struggle
To enrich the beauties they were born with;

Often we call Sublime that which rises above
Frailty into godliness; how many heavens have we therefore
Leveled the world into! The feeble man ascends slightly,
Tho' it is much for him: therefore how godly he is!
The fool is once a sage: therefore how godly he is!
The malformed man has a balanced spirit: how godly!
The cruel becomes merciful: therefore how godly!
O nothing blinds more than the proportioning of godliness;

No; we must not allow pity for the struggle
To cloud our appraisal of the struggle's end result,
Else pity will overwhelm all striving and endeavor,
And all potential will be encouraged to fail,
And all hope will drowse in a lullabied self-satisfaction
That teaches our souls nothing more than to love ourselves
For the flaws with which we were born.

IV. Admiration and Encumbrance

Truly, admirers ruin beauty by their admiration,
Encouraging what is pretty to them to remain the same
And delight them the same; and so they dwarf
By imprisoning in their own too-little soil
The flowers they ought to compel
To drink in the sun and the earth to the highest;
But so it is; always the Unremarkable
Would seek to keep heaven low.

Thus they who love the Beautiful
Burden the Beautiful, perverting the purpose
Of beauty in men by emboldening beautiful men
To believe that Being alone is triumph enough, and to forget
How poorly plain beauty embodies the Idyllic, and to never discover
That the world is not divided into those who have much
And those who have little, but those who make much or little

Of what they have.

I shall not pity the Beautiful;
Beauty is desirable, and so draws
Admiration, and admiration corrupts;
And corruption is merely to love oneself
Unreasonably;

And yet, to the beast in others, to those
Who by the beast in themselves are overcome,
Is beauty, however noble,
Forever bound.

[Orpheus]

The shroud of prescience.

'Twas a voice that woke me as I slept
And bid me gaze, as they slipped past us, down
Into the frill of the silver waters. There was nothing,
Only my shadow and the shadow of the ship
Cast by the high pale goddess throned massively
Above the finger of the mast, - but there was nothing,
Only the steady murmur of the sea against our shell,
The call, the cry, the coo - plashing - of the sea.

And yet what stirs there? - no - yes, those were eyes!
Flashing in the wake that curled away;
There for a moment, glimmer of flames,
Then fluttered and were gone; but then again
They sparked to life, and away from them
Some curved form lengthened, some large fleshy body
Tapering to a gently writhing end silently waved
Its strange bulk in the moonlight, then sank away.

Had that been the end of it, I might have called it
A dream. But after long gazing into silence
There came suddenly a voice, and lowering my eyes
Steeply down to the sea beneath me I saw, very formlessly,
A face, hazed as if by smoke beneath the sliding sea-shroud,
Whose bright eyes burned with golden fire, kelp locks green
As emerald filaments rinsing, as I watched, his godly flesh;
And slowly into the dim light there rose a strong neck
And magnificent shoulders, sinewed to the flare of perfect arms
And the big drum of a god's chest, falling thence
From shining skin to shimmering scales which dwindled like a flame
Down into the depths, swaying as they darkened . . .

And as I sat transfixed by his bizarre beauty,
He spoke in a voice that flowed
Like breakers when their rage is spent to peace unfolded,
When with a lowly purl they wrinkle back
Beneath the face of the deep.

[Glaucos]

Wraith.

Deep in the night he opened his eyes
On a full moon framed by leaves,
And a pleasant voice, long-unheard,
Long-awaited, whose young sprightly lilts
Still nimbly spry beneath the fallen crests of his intonations,
Chimed with what they'd once made buoyant by making lucid, -
And his heart surged, but his body lay frozen, and he found
That no matter how he strained he could not stir his limbs, which lay
Just as he'd fallen into slumber, braced on a great stone's
Velvet moss, all in flowers beside a pooling spring;
And as he watched, a dark figure rose in the night
From the shadows of the fountain before him,
Like a specter, rose to full outline on the bank
And spoke, shrouded in the gloom of the trees.

[Endymion]

In fountain water she bath'd.

On nothing so lovely
As a lake in the noon of night
Has ever the daystar thrust his garish fires;
The tremble of the crystal, shudder of flesh
Throbbing with rainbows' footfalls, till the soft waters
Loosed from strife settle, contused, into the evening,
And calming to a deep deep sleep smooth
To a glass, glint of stars, sheen of a smoldering moon;

And I am a bather in the lake of the night,
The deep night, the dark night, the pure soft mirror
Lapsing into caverns of icy moonbeams, trembling into blackness;
And this is fear: to float on the liquid face of nothing;
And this is doubt: to feel the base of a depth,
Without your eyes to show you what is there;

The moon, in the silence, comes through you,
Carries you beyond yourself below and below . . .
You think of the forest, the dense, the mingle below
Of frond and stone, above of star and lordly flower,
The fog-dense midnight, close of the caverns
Of green-brushed light, lurk of disfigured beasts
Whose bane is worse than death; O fear itself
Is a depth of shadows, sprung of dreams, sprung
Of everything's nebulous opposite that never can truly
Manifest in the grow of things, not when only
The down of death is the vilest low;

O were I a lover I would fear
To inflict my death on my beloved;
But that is love; lovers must suffer it;
Yet I, I have not tied my heart to another,
And I am not wrong to care nothing
If nothing must live on lower in itself
To be less for the loss of me;
I falter below, and am lost
To only myself . . .

And that is freedom.

O hear me, cold stars:
I forgot my fear of the forest when I saw
That all that a forest can do to a man
Is make him sleep.

[Hylas]

I saw you fondly coveting long life.

Deep in the bellies of streams there are golden halls,
Whose columns are sunshafts or beams of moon,
Whose domes are blue by day and silver by night,
Whose splendor is all in gold and diamond, walls like sapphire
Banners in wind, ethereally beautiful . . .

Is this heaven, that shines with lust and greed?
And are these gods, who take away the pains of desire?
There is pleasantry below, delight as has never sighed
So blissfully in any hall of human opulence or valor,
Like a dream unceasing its sweetness to pour over, overwhelm,
And carry off to a sweeter other, forgetting the last,
Like a river to cleanse and disremember,
And to animate with every pleasure
The fresh and strange and never-felt.

O father, know that I did not willingly abandon you,
And I do not find these deep lush hidden heavenly bowers
More desirable than a lifetime of struggling with you
Together at your side;

But have you thought that the greatest human love
May be reached through misery, - a misery all for love,
Suffered for love, a willing sacrifice, for love?
I had thought so, very deeply, I had thought it was the only way, -
No other path to what we most desire than devotion,
Devotion to make us worthy of, to make us strong enough for, love,
Bent tho' we are by so many leanings-away;

But O their hands are ivory! Curls of mist, they reach
And brush aside the streaming stars!
Water like sky above me, they laugh at how the beauty of things
Astounds me, and something in the way they instantly seize
What is fine to them has put the curious thought in my mind
That they do not pause to contemplate love and beauty
Because they do not fear never finding them;

And I think we know what we desire,
Only when we know we cannot find it again.

[Heracles]

Is death alike, then, to the young and old?

O stars you will not aid me? O Moon?
Have I earned nothing's love or admiration,
Most you, O Moon, full as you are,
Cannot stand taller in the sky to guide me as I thrust
To the netherworld of this deepest water,
Whose dim nadir may summit soundless,
Beyond the spread of the body that breathes?

He spoke, then fled like a shadow; the dark pool
Untremblingly lay as tho' he had not stood there,
Had not stepped up among the reed-shades, and spoken
In his so-familiar voice words that were undoubtedly his;
Yet tunneling blindly I found black deepness only, -
No land at bottom, only the earth, the air, the night
To re-ascend to, the silence of only myself
Measuring a blank depth, floundering in a void,
Feeling eyelessly for an end.

Lower, lower, lower, till gazing behind
I saw the silver portal of the world
Orb to a little eye, then blink to a little star,
Then seem like not the world; that portal of the world
Where now 'tis night and stars preside, and a moon,
That great thing withered to a little star, -
Is that a world to us? that house of our love being, clearly,
Barely a teardrop on the face of nothing, and surely no beading of
Anguish or sympathy tumbling from the eye
Of an ashamed and melancholic God . . .

A moment's feeling, deep in the lonely silence,
Caught between an unseeable love and the shadowy world
I lengthen downward to lift him back to . . .
                    At last, overcome! Conquered!
            Conquered by the ceaseless gloom
I released, gave up, surrendered, fell away,
Hardly feeling that I rose or plummeted,
Till winking into life that small globe budding above me

Proved ascension, and the light of it grew and grew
And grew and grew to surround me,
Me, husk, me, lover of light, pulled beyond resistance,
As very weakly I yearned to prolong myself
Deep in the abyss, pulled me, limp, defeated,
Through the silver threshold of the world of moons and stars.

[Daidalos]

Such law from nature receiv'd I not.

Was it out of mere disobedience, or something more,
That either he to the sun or the sun to he
Spoke some charming overwhelming words,
And put the desire for the Highest in his spirit,
And in the intoxication of his freedom swept him like a wild dream
Over the slow reluctant numbness-loving part of his soul
To chase to the height of the light of the world
His heart's most golden desire?

And he looked directly into the sun and the pure white fire
Broke the boundaries of his vision, and his eyes burst
For too much seeing and his heart burst
For Beauty's overflow and last his soul which was all of him
Collapsed like a heavy star and erupted across the heavens . . .

For none shall say it was not a vast death, no,
Say it was not a cosmic aspiration . . .
But shall we all go die big deaths? All try for an hour
Of godliness to put our human parts to shame
Till the world say, *Let us praise the self-immolator,*
Who threw his golden body into the sun!

[Orpheus]

Abandonment. The bay.

He came down out of the mountains to the shore
And weakly trod the shingle down
To where the waves beat the sand,
And setting one knee to the cool drawn beach paused;

There the tide lay long and low, the tired waves
Lapping lightly, lightly, and lightlier were
Drawn away; and the blood-red sky melting,
Dying sun bleeding his last through mountains
Of blushing cloud, and goldenly the long path lay
Shimmering on the sea;

He felt the small waves touch and fall away;
                    Touch, and fall away;
The cold sea rose around his weary hands, knees, feet like sweet relief
            And was gone again,
And rose again, and again, gone away . . .

And lightlier rose each rise,
And lightlier fell each fall,
Until the sea had sunk away to the sun
And left him lonely on the sand . . .

[Heracles]

Far from the hour of white horses.

The soft waves lap the shore;
The soft grass sways and is silent again;
And the soft wind sighs, and the soft moon glows,
And the breakers die in rings of softer flows, -

From the hills' and woodlands' hidden hollows
Unseen creatures softly pulse their rhythms,
And softly one still-singing fair-voiced night-melodian
Rings his clear notes on the moon-cool air . . .

And all this music rises,
Rises to the stillness of the stars . . .
All is hushed, for the night
Is gentler than the day, is a time
Of softer melody, and of day-covered rhythm
Unveiled and sounded to the fore;
Indeed, my footsteps seem a trespass, -
This forest floor, roaring with the noise
Of my impressions upon its frail dewy flowers, grasses and leaves,
Would sound so less harshly if 'twere only yon graceful moon's beams
Feathering their beautiful light upon its frailty, -
But I must tread here, and I must
Break this night and every night's meditation
With deep long cries for him I've lost; for I have shouted
To the dark echoing distances his name, and again, his name, and again;
And no reply has come.

What do I seek, what sign do I search for?
I know his voice calling back and he waiting in the next glade onward
Would end my searchings, my sorrows, - but when, as now,
The hope of so sweet a culmination has gone from the light
Of not-impossible expectation, what hope follows?
What do I look for, if not he?
And if he is gone and lost forever,
What other faith in what other man or calling can eclipse
The affectionate rays of the leaping young sun he was for me?
And his affection was not like so many others who claim to love me,

Who love me only for my name and strength and eminence for great deeds,
Yet do not love what does not labor for them;
His was a purer devotion.

O night, I see now how soft and how shy
And how silent you are, seeing you alone, -
I've known cities too much, and companions,
And deeds worth endless lives in song
Have seemed everything to me, as gods, we deem,
Love what they admire, and over them nothing reigns;
But you are still; you sleep, caring nothing of me;
You mock, you laugh with my own voice, circling my broken griefs
To clear derisions, so that I'm struck by what I weep, -
Your serenity, so indifferent to the awful commotion
Of the things men live and die for, is humbling
Because you are so vast, and wonderful, and strange, -
This, I suppose, is why by most you're slept through,
That as you hardly speak and yet yawn open unfathomable depths
Of uncertainty and darkness and doubt you resolve nothing
Your limitless calm calls into question, and you satisfy nothing
Of earthly virtue or godliness, neither hating nor loving,
But seemingly beyond both hatred and love.

This taunts mortality, that hates how much like death
Eternity seems, that would age like stars but scorn slow movement,
That cannot bear its short life nor the patient silence of moments
Slowed to starlight to make them centuries, beyond what can be suffered
By a thing of sense and still maintain that sanity
That lives briefly and boldly enough for human love.

So much is said when words are nothing,
And I see how the night might say
That life is a fire that fades into ashes
And is ashes thereafter, and they spread;
And I see how the night might say
That life is day and death is night,
That sheds to apathy coherence, vision, and faith;
And I see how the night might say
That this is what we become when we cease to be men,
And so life is beautiful, as are men,
When life's daylight sustains them;

And I see that there is life here
Only if by loving it we make it so;
Not wise enough am I to know this,
But I think there may be wisdom
In loving till love devours us,
And thus may ours be the loveliest ends.

Ah, but that . . . that is pitiless;
And you, O night, now you speak,
And there is no softer wisdom;

For you sing the peace of death;
And not that death that's best for lovers, tho' they're
Broken by it, but that long ocean love vainly desires
That rolls on and on and on till its waters widen into sand
And the winds spread and the sun melts into the moon, into the stars,
And the stars melt too and glow no longer, and everything
That can grow has grown and will not again, and words have
Withered to silence as less and less was there to oppose
What words convey of less-obvious truths;
And could love suffer the slow infinity of this
It would become this way itself and spread this way, spreading apart,
And love would change to something different, less like falling, more like
        firm stars
That hold one another as they slowly dance and love would change
To a starful sky that's slowly slowly danced through would change
To every star uncoiling and diluting into every other star would thin
To a dull glow and thin and thin
And thin and thin and thin
To nothing;

But that is not how humans love.

[Admetos]

To cross clear waters.

I.

Is this love: to fear love's end?
More than the bliss of a lifetime, to fear
The sudden absence of a life that always kept death off
By holding heaven near, my philosophy of life, near and true, -
I fear not that youth decays, but that love's end is built
Through love's beginnings, that very sad beauty-in-consolation
As we use what held us most to life to ease our leaving it,
As tho' to marshal spring against the rest,
To make the parting less . . .

       O but how to resist
The Heaven of Reunions, Heaven of Innocence,
Fresh snow of love, spotless, free, outside of the laws of the world, -
How to keep old love from collapsing into a dream of youth,
That youth be so desired as to convince the mind of anything,
Of anything so long as love ends restored, not reconciled,
Not reconciled to anything less than what one remembers holding,
Tho' memory may even tinge it with an over-beauty not once there;

And why is that so terrifyingly sad? That some beautiful figure
Of some long-vanished once-loved tenderness
Can re-surface, tearing the heart it helped to build?
Memories of love, to suffer them knowing them lost,
Comfort finds only in more than mere memories'
Resurrection; but that is the widower's burden;
More grievous, tho', the burden borne by both, as,
Leaving their partnership perhaps forever, they must
From death and life wring consolation, life for the dying,
Life for the living, life for both beyond that looming division;
How sad and beautiful to pillow a heart's departure
With slumberous sweet fantasies that they depart
For a land of lovers' dreams.

II.

O the clear flowing loveliness of the waters
Whose purity I dare not step across unclean;
Face on the fair stream, what have you corrupted?
To promise death rises into love and joy, to aspire,
To hope for this, have I lied that her heart might hand itself
More calmly over to interminable sleep? What right have I
To make eternal oaths, guess at some absurd longevity
That plainly stands incongruous with everything
Life brings us to understand;

And yet I . . . somehow I find
That nothing is lowered by sympathy,
But is raised to the height of the flaw it mends, -
So the whole earth mourns a breaking, a broken heart,
And the innocence of things makes them divinely armed
To succor us when reason gives life rocks
When life needs meadows, -

For I am the teller of impossible tales,
The maker of impossible promises;
Not a liar, only a fool trying to keep his lips to his love's;
I merely voiced the dream we both desired;
But the most heartbreaking vision of all
Was that she believed.

So I give you waters a prayer now,
Penance for a thoughtlessness performed for love;
You rinse, cold strain, these hands of adulteration,
Diminish with their soil crystallinely away . . .

And I pass on without new woe.

[Orpheus]

Gazing into the flood.

. . . He lifted his eyes to the near sea
And saw that there floated some dim thing
Limply in the surf;
                          And at once a great hope
                    Welled up in his heart,
                          And then fell at once
          To a deeper sadness,
And then deeper to a deep deep dread
That here may lie drowned and broken his heart's
Once-lovely attendant, and association so adored . . .

But there is the face, half-sunken, so pale and so lovely,
The face of another youth; how bizarre and grotesque,
How beautiful he is! like some stone-molded man
Fallen from some god's citadel on blue heaven's
Cloud-duned shore, he is ethereal;
Serenely he nods in the warbling rollers;
He gazes on eternity with one pale eye.

[Heracles]

Prayer. Cleansing of soil.

On the ocean,
Reflection of a god's beauty;

In defiance of the gravid, he had both man's and bird's freedom;
Man's soul knows limits, dismays at the body's burden,
Longs to throw the body off, be light like a bird;
Indeed no god lies broken here, only a boy, who lived and grew
And every dawn woke unrenewed, therefore different,
And sacred for the change;

He floats on rainbow plumes: is it true?
That Man has made wings for himself, despite his heaviness?
I see in the pale bloodless beauty of his impassive face
The excess of furious defiance that once undoubtedly spoke
In the blush and pluck and the stormy beating
Of a soul that radiated outward like a prism
When struck by the beautiful rays of a new freedom, -
These thin wings indeed must spread from the pivot of some big heart
That burned free of a too slight and meltable frame,
Fell bursting in flames, was doused in the sea;
Whatever god gapes his apathetic jaws to swallow such falling stars
Is no lover of what is tremendous in the soul,
But devours only and devours and devours,
And knows neither End nor Goal;

Dead boy, your mortality makes you beautiful;
Like some beauteous bird burned up by the jealous gods
For flashing free wings on heaven's threshold of silver glass,
You lie there, too lovely to be a corpse;
Both father and mother, child, to your own godliness!
More than a pitiful man, and less than a languorous god,
Did you will this? Did you will so much defiance, so contradictory
To the impulse for long sheltered life, so calmly hollow now,
As tho' the soul once covered here threw this cloak-of-a-body off
And caught fire to live in heaven as a roaming star;

Perhaps not; I cannot believe in a god
Whose supremacy is so dear to him
That he burns up thunderousness in men
When they happen to be
                    Reverberant;
        If any god indeed could love
He would not love even the sun or the ocean;
O you are a feeble dream, man-made-fiery-heaven-strider,
And only a very young god, born human and at the outset
Of his immortality, would find sympathy in his dissolving heart
For this flower of only one of infinite springs.

Come, child, I will bury you with my own hands;
Nothing can terrify you now, I know this,
But let us find for you some earthier shelter than the sea
To slumber in, the sea whose heartless maws would soon
Consume you entirely, tho' I shall salvage you
To save myself the thought of all this lovely human glory
Gorged on as you slide raggedly
Into so many abyssal throats;

I am a fool to believe I do anything more than this.
God, perhaps, is not what whitely eddies in these eyes;
He could very well be, I fear, an appellation only
Of vague Fear countered by the human sense
Of necessary Justice;

So no, no, he did not will this;
Bedraggled, wrecked, beaten, broken;
To will such a thing was beyond him.

[Orpheus]

Bathe them, composer, in sweetly-flowing water.

Once more we cast our eyes
On erstwhile loves;

We have danced in goldened vales
Of the sun's last light before he slumbers,
And we have sung to the silent valleys hung with stars;
We cling to the earth, cling to the moon, to the sky,
Not as havens always reached for, nor as youth desiring
Heavens of youth, but rather as lilts of memory
Once merely hills and meadows, moments,
Far lights caught rippling in the flood, -
Heavenward weep the willows of our reachings,
And dawn glowing in the crystal blue
Shivers the somber clinging rains
To vibrancy.

Never by the world is love forsaken,
Never is hope unrequited by an end to sprouting suns;
All, suffering through deaths of dormancy, returns to us,
Reformed in infinite ways but drawing us by intimations
Back to the cherished days we lovingly yearn for,
And there is no wound the world cannot redeem
By growing through, and growing over . . .

Much have we lost, and heartache speaks
That men do not come back like flowers;
Rose and daffodil, nameless, wordless, deedless,
Grow and wither, unique only for their age
Along the curve of bloom, and tho' we mourn their going,
No endless griefs enclose in fruitless earth
Our sorrows' knells, and we rest our endless faith
On days to come, undoubting springs will kindle again
Cold hearts and beds of rest;

But men we grieve as gone, and dam our
Floods of tears with lovely idyll dreams
Of meadowed heavens that mother the beloved dead

To new and better life;

But soon we find, beyond the roll of,
Toll of days, we find love cannot suffer
Sunshine and satiation to the end of time, -
And life, we see, is not life without life's partings.

Brothers,
Darkly bury nothing in the earth
That flies away still lovely.
Many things are meadows, and all reflowers
Vaguely in remembered form, but never the same
As drowned in the shadow of the fall;
Whatever of dawn or evening was reveille
To a moment of love, we call upon,
And shiver the sad rains to mist in the morning sun.

[Admetos]

And let her go beneath the earth.

I.

The cold form pales
Of one I loved, the warm blood drains
Of life and soul, the body wilts, the heartbeat slows,
And all she was dies with the tender vital flow, -
To behold a love departing, dissolving away,
A loss beyond recall, a lover gone,
Forever gone away;
Past hope, the desperate soul may say,
To the chill unloving wind may say,
To where does all the loveliness go?

Once were birdsongs warbled in the night,
And seemed to sing the song of you and me;
Then we to theirs enjoined our lay of love's
Abiding joy, and in those moments knew the agelong
Truth of what all lovers think, believe, and say:
That lovers fade, but love forever stays.

II.

O to the stars I loved you! And down
              To the bed of the sea!
          Above the love I bore for my own life,
      The love I bore for yours,
And that the light may once more forth from those fair windows
Wherethrough spoke in smiles the loveliest of all souls,
I would live what life remains to me
Buried in the dark earth's barrow,
Forgotten by all but one whose love is most to me,
If thus to live would set you breathing again
Beneath the sun's warm glow;
Even then, this broken heart would ail me less, -
I see 'tis but a living death awaits me now;
I know not yet how I shall live;
If I thrive at all in days to come, it shall not be

By the natural rains that I am fed, but rather
By the beautiful tears I see you weeping
As you wait for me on some far shore, -
      Tears that only the dead may shed,
      And only the living, adore.

III.

O what springs have I lost, that I had hoped for!
How abruptly the dream ends, waking to a life so dull and slow
And dreary; I feel to the right and find no answering hand,
No warmth to purr familiarly beneath a caress,
Nothing of that contact that eased wonderfully
Along the svelte camber of a lovely human life,
Pausing at the soft isthmus where the soft life beat
Between the head and the heart;

I had wished to follow you, - had wished
To follow you until an ending far
Took you or me unwillingly away, away . . .
What we have always feared, what made love fierce
Between us, fear that one would fade
Before the dream is out, before love's rivers
Have carried us off the whole great length of the sky
To the setting dawn, to where an ending
And a drifting off is desirable
To sink to the sweetest softest closing
Those twin journeys of love and life;

O life! O life is nothing without you,
For you were love! Love only
Can bring this heartless world
Down calmly to peace,
Dissolving the fairest illusions
To a truth that wrinkles down
In golden folds, to an insight
Last unfurled.

IV.

What was it that you loved?
The eyes of green, or the woman in the eyes?
Once you were young, and beauty was everything,
Even so far as to cloud all else, all else . . .
All else worthier, indeed, than even the wildest
Pleasures that bodies can churn;
Youth hopes to find that union of ideal
Fairness and perfect grace that will *give* love always
As love is given, perfect bond of being and being
Whose love, each in each, leaves nothing to be desired.

Olive eyes, - do they spark love?
Love is devotion, - do they spark devotion?
Devotion is endless, - so was she life to you?
Was she so much nourishment that her death
Has doomed you now to bitter dearth, as tho'
The sky has withered with her lovely face, or the sun
Obscured with her lovelier eyes, or the body of the earth
Made barren, or lakes, streams, oceans dried and winds
All laid because her final breath has blown
And settled to silence, -

O was she life to you, as water is life?
Or was she something more, that does not
Make you die or keep you living, if living
Is only to last, bough-grasp, stay fresh,
Mellow toward fruition;
For nothing is of use to us, seasons of being
Being bare if we bury our ripeness or unripeness
Or overripeness under the canopy, and never allow
Green eyes and then a tender hand to search for us,
Take hold of us, break us away, open us up;
We decay, yes, but at least are desired;
The blessing of air and light, taste, fragrance,
Ourselves cracked, broken in the hands of another;
Heart-cloven, and yet without this
We would wither without use.

V.

Embracing me she whispered, *Never be dust . . .*
And kissed my eyes and shed soft tears against my heart,
And spoke sadly between sighs of death's shadow
Looming always over love, and of the loneliness of lovers
Left behind, and of her wish to never live to see my death,
So never to be reft of my heart to love her;
For once I told her how the purity of immolation pleased me,
The utter release of it, the shedding, the full surrendering
Of my body to the world; for I thought the farewell less
To have the shell of me thus thinned to thwart decay,
That the thought of all my warmth now cold and moldering
Would do more damage to her living heart than the pure
And final discharge of one unimaginably painful
But liberating moment;

And yet my words brought only tears to her eyes,
And a quiet request that she voiced out of the melancholy
Of a far-off desolation; for she asked that should I die
My body not be burned to ashes, but laid whole
Into the womb of the earth, never to make her bear the gray ruins
Of the arms and the chest and the eyes that loved her,
And the hands and the lips that caressed and loved her,
But that they lower me to my unwaking rest
In some ageless bed of a meadow, where still would remain
The vessel of my heart not far below this very lovable
Living portion of the earth which has that gift
Of making of the shed blood of rained desolation
Unnumbered new breathing beautiful organs of life;

And the heart will say:
In spring I shall come with the meadow,
In summer and autumn age in the meadow,
Decline to the droop of the dusk of the meadow,
Fray to the young-dying sun, fold inward, sleep deeply,
And arrive bearing branches of a love-gift of fruit-flowers,
        Young in the meadow;

And into the seasons of life her faith will lose its grief,
Tears that green eyes weep to the green world,
The hope that a single tear might slowly crawl below
To be the grace that nourishes me;
Her love, she said, in how she saw me last
Might find its peace, not as a wind-blown man-unmade
Without vestige even of figure, of color, of aroma,
But buried as I loved her, that not at once
But slowly I would leave her, this my body gradually
Fading in her mind, where always, below the bend
Of a familiar tree, or the tremble of an intimate flower,
At least a part of our love not utterly borne away
Might lie bodily, yet human in the earth,
Love's breast of fire cooled
But never abolished.

VI.

Songbird sing your full heart open!
To love we must have song to grant love's
Pleasant bonds of grace to the bays between us,
Through all the decay that makes us earthly, everlasting,
Strong vulnerable earthly songs, full of body,
Never borne all at once in once in one day's man or woman;
We find our loves perfect
Only when we find them in our past.

What is this love I feel in you,
These lovely blending bleeding colors
You spin from air? The world around my heart
Has drawn before as now again I closely twine
To this little trill she would have lovingly heard
As a ballad to tender feeling, and a call to intimacy and devotion,
And in this song and all birdsongs henceforth
This quality shall ring.

Heaven on earth, you shy sweet vulnerable girl,
Blind to your own beauty, -
You hate yourself for what is frail and imperfect in you,
Tho' I love you most because you know how imperfect you are,
And yet still can live joyfully in this world of tremendous beauty,

Perishing peacefully hand in hand with the eternal beauty and youth
Of men's and flowers' generations . . .

Had I so serene converse with eternal nature around me
I might feel that we are still together, bound by
Mutual love for things outside of our souls that last forever,
And I could believe that love for a man or a woman
Could endure with us, as the world endures, as we love
What they made of the world, and what for ourselves
The world became through them.

VII.

Bury the girl
In a sea of flowers, -
Lay meadows beneath her
And meadows above her,
Weave her, wed her, join her,
Spring to spring;

For heaven to live one day is not too little,
Nor from Time's youth to undying diffusion
Is a heaven's eternal flowering
Lovelier than men's blue days.
A single sway of sun,
Rose rising, purple parting day,
Unfurling sapphiring spreads arms lily-glorious
From morning's fragile heart . . .

And O the turn of hours, curve of flowers
As they list to the lean of the light!
And they are essential, even when they curve
And wither and slowly die, if only to prove
That a flower always ends the way it bloomed.

[Heracles]

May no god be envious.

I.

There is the pale shining path
Across the sea, the softly trembling sea,
The waves that softly beat the silver shore,
The dark low luster of the sand beneath,
And not a cloud above to veil the gleaming
Of a sky of silent stars that softly burn . . .

O how fair to feel the soft winds flow,
The quiet woods, the quiet moonlight
Hovering on lagoons, how they wander
In obsidian stillness the dim shorelength,
Sad derelicts of an abandoning tide;
And there, holding heaven above the ocean,
Wavering high in white quiet luster, still sparks
Gradually leap from an unseen stoked sun;

We say: A man may seek what he has lost.
To the end of him, his wholeness maimed by many losses,
A man will search the deepness of his heart
For the moments and the faces, the songs and the visions,
That planted in his soul a love for his life, and a love for living.
Tho' the world will empty of the things he loves, it will remain
That once he loved those things that now are gone;
It is the love, the love that stays, -
Tho' They left, enriching him forever,
Lovely yet and living in him,
And tho' They forsook him,
Shed him, cast him off,
          Fair was the parting;
Reluctantly and full of love They took their leave.

O yes there is a pain in every parting,
And a beauty inherent only to the ends of things;
And yet we must . . . yet must we live, yes, . . .
But cannot live and believe in nothing;

Larger purposes, common faiths,
Anthem-fervors, drumbeat-beliefs,
Insular senseless iniquitous fanaticisms;
No, not these, not these at all;
Merely something in the sway of things
That we rely on, honesty to that;
Else death would be the heaven of our desires.

                    And so,
To whatever god governs the love of lost loveliness:
          I surrender.

II.

It is a sad thing to leave being human behind,
Like losing a part of ourselves we cherish
And yet we know is frail, to part with
That sympathy that makes us love our limitations
When those impotences make us vulnerable
To the tragic rift rebuffing our capacities
From seizing our desires;

For nothing grows by holding on too much
To what it has been, and as to love as humans love
Is to withhold ourselves by holding on to what has held us,
There must be something in the balance of memory
And forgetfulness that makes our beauty more
Than death, which is the one, and gods,
Which are the other;

And O I thank God I am not eternal!
You gods who lie hidden beneath all things
Who so arrogantly now preside over mortal infirmity,
Taking what you desire, deceiving, laughing, destroying
Whatever men can build in their briefness;
There will come a time for something godlier than laughter,
When all men staidly lie in the only blissful bower you cannot reach,
You will some unspeakable day disentomb them,
Furious at how patiently they have accepted their lifelessness,
Only to find that they have vanished even from their graves!
And you are left alone, devoid of any far-off culmination

Of your long eternal meditations on ideals and hopeless hopeful
Dreams, that never within them bear even the slightest possibility
Of materializing in some divergent reality
Beyond the one existence they grew from;
O I thank God I am not eternal!

Man is such that yearning becomes him,
A yearning balanced by a running-away of desire
That does not falsely culminate in his own passing;
No, no . . . yearning is not yearning that does not end
In either love or silence, and they both have their beauties . . .
You, father of a son, yearn for inadequacy;
I, childless, yearn for totality;
Till when this dreaded task of yearning
Shall close on truth, and I shall *know*
And not be afraid.

Not easily do we bid farewell to the past,
And live, tho' letting go,
Of much of what gave us life.
Love ignores what death will do to it,
And love is thus so wise to blind our hearts
Lest fear of loss appall our loveliest bonds.

IV

F A R E W E L L

CLARIFICATION *of* CONTEXT

ICAROS observes his father building; how his father tells him stories as he works; the fable of King Syrophanes, whose memorial to his deceased young son haunts him with grief;

Apollo grieves the dead Hyacinthos, a young man whom he had loved, as he bleeds in the meadow; how the young man had accidentally perished as he attempted to catch a discus thrown by the god, and was instead struck by it; how the boy's body vanishes into the earth, which then erupts with magnificent flowers; and how the earth's gift is comforting to Apollo;

The dialogue of Hylas and the nymphs; how Heracles, hearing a birdsong in the forest, finds therein a solace; and the hero resigns himself to fate of his child, sets off to meet what shall befall him in days to come;

How Admetos rests beneath a tree to watch the approaching dawn; his thoughts drift on another dawn; how, expecting the sun to rise, he wakes to rather find himself in his bedchamber, and the moon has barely advanced beyond its full zenith;

Endymion desires eternal sleep, finding that only in dreams can he lie together with his love; the appeal of Death; the appeal of Sleep; how Endymion's wish is granted by the king of gods; and the world falls away; the pale moon eddies to an eye.

[Icaros]

Buried thoughts.

There were at first
The hollow frames, hung from strings,
And he with nimble fingers spinning out the wispy wood,
Slow spider, composing his lucid intricacies;
And then the soft wax, which I would knead delightedly
Between my fingers, so smooth and pliant it was;
And with what seemed to me unfathomable patience
He laid out the feathers in descending fashion,
Large tapering to small, and mounted them to the curved,
The latticed reeds;

And as they flushed to fullness, I below would wait
For a breeze to wake in them delicate ripples,
Like wind on tranquil water, how they
Skim and settle, echo the unrest;
Barely a breeze-breath and the pearl feathers shook and ruffled,
Broke the sunlight to colors, flooded the floor and walls
And high-domed ceiling, made them rollick with colorful light . . .

And that was how the days went, - one below,
One above; often, in the evenings,
When fell the golden sun against the sea,
The dusk-beams streaming through the narrow windows
Would shimmer on the liquid wings and wash that dark hollow,
Sink it into an ocean of twinkling lights;

Then by candlelight into the deep silent evenings
He worked, and I below would wait for a feather to fall, -
And there was silence so deep that I could hear in the half-light above me
The click of wooden skeletons assembling, of wax becoming sinew,
The ruffling and the soft steady breaths which, always so evenly cadenced,
Set my heart at ease; and as he worked he would, in his gentle way,
Recount for my delight the histories of ancient deities,
The love of mortal for immortal, immortal for mortal,
How sad that love is, how rarely is attained desired permanence
Or fleetingness desired, how much more is love
Than only desire, the death for one, life for another,

Of love unreturned, the failure of immortality to win
The mortal spirit, and that love needs far less than forever
To feel the eternity of a devoted heart, how death is death
More to the living, who always forget how content
The dead are, how fully themselves the dead are
Regardless of their life's desires obtained or not obtained,
Forgotten or not forgotten, that they are content
Because beyond them, so very far beyond them
That fulfillment is a buried thought, deeply buried
Lover's impetus baffling the heart that breaks itself
And cannot wholly mend, the blessing of forgetfulness
And the heart at last lain beyond life's griefs;

And he mounted a further feather;

And sending down his voice from somewhere among
His splendid creations, which mingled their rustle
With his words, lovely-dark his sad melodies, the sad
Melancholy mumblings of his heart, and the little shadowy fable
Of the old king in the early days of the world whose young beloved son
Perished still a child, and how unwilling to abandon his fled first hope,
Adorned his palace with his effigy;
                              And how
The shadow of him day by day brought only youth
To his desolation, brought no healing to his heart, and he thought
How very godlike it must be to find oneself each day renewed,
Renewed of the fading and unfading memories of some mortal fragment
One saw slip to oblivion; and he would say that men are men
Because they live briefly enough to love distinctly
And beautifully suffer, and gods are gods
Because they do not turn their losses
To grief.

So he would say, and align another feather.

[Syrophanes]

Idos dolu, the appearance of grief.

Is that you, Grief, there in the darkness,
Half-shadowed? How can you grin, how was I
Blind so much to wish you hammered back to life?
Life's likeness, dead appearance of a loss,
Embittering to barrenness the bare deserts
Of our once-voiceful-now-windswept attachment;
You grinning ghost, laughing, perfect,
Out of the shade of memory; you clear effigy
In the sunlight, boy in the moon, sometimes I hear
A laughter in the night's cold noon, yet look to find you
Placid, touch-cool, as you always are now;
Sometimes I glimpse the movement of an eye,
Tilt of a hand or smile's glow, then approach, absurd,
To find them twinkles of the herb-embers blushing
As they gradually writhe to cinders at your feet,
And then my sorrows find their youth.

Memorial, memory, token of a memory;
I thought that love was to have you always
Before me, in spite of fate and all that fate can take
Away beyond us, for all that stays is faith.

Faith, you, thrusting there a cold and glittering face
To the dew-gray channels of the moon, haunt me;
God, fiend, dream, monster, - laugh, glimmer - demon, hope, specter,
          wraith;
All except what made you you, everything perfectly laid out
To make more death of death, and to make death more and greater
Than a fleet parting that ever and ever runs away from us,
That even might trail out to a life that does not fall
To utter grief, forgetting how their love could never desire
To harm us simply for living, knowing how life crumbles
More for those who live, how death is not unlike a voyage off
Over the mountains to a land of endless meadows
That stretch away forever, and is to always be beginning that journey,
And always forgetting what has already been seen and passed and died
With the moment, and to always be free of the malaise of explorers,

Who finding nothing tire of the quest and long for home,
But always to be those first hopes, those setting-off-ideals,
Those moments of first discovery that will go on to form
The clearest and most heart-warming-breaking memories,
And to know not what is supposed to be found, beyond the thrill
Of one new sight of beauty beyond another, beyond another, beyond
Another vision overwhelming to the man-made burden of grief
That we bear because we cannot allow the world to be larger than us
And to move completely in its own artless sphere that is yet kind enough
To be beautiful as we live and as we die and after we die within it,
And tho' it knows nothing of kindness yet holds more
Of kind and beautiful sentiments than all our art has ever feigned
A knowledge of, we blind conquerors who claim everything
And release only the ruins of it, lovers who turn everything
To sadness, fathers and mothers of so much self-deceiving greed
That everything we come to desire we chain to ourselves,
And will not let free to be the fullest freest love, -

Rains will never once more fill this, but heaven will slowly
Drink these waters off, so slowly they will hardly seem to go at all,
Like the moonbeams as they slide very slowly off his face
And leave him fully in the darkness, he goes;

And then I think of far-flung springs, of inchoation,
Of the hawthorn altar to innumerable healing hearts
Whose pale soft flowers rock and waver in the wind;
But then I think how he is gone,
And all of this fades.

[Apollo]

Hyacinthos. What charm, what potent hand?

I.

This coil of laurels, writhe of florets and folioles
Whorled to a crown adorns me, ever green, evokes
Young gardens not yet forgotten, their bloom, their beauty,
Their promise; and how unwilted they took their place above me,
Not the greenwoods ageless I had wished for, not the flowers
Every season, but fixed in this garland of memory's delight,
Live on.

Not everything is certain; even I , who thought to be as a father is
To a child of the earth, chose not to cast my thoughts ahead
To learn the path of our affection, too much fearing
A shadow over everything we might have done . . .
It is hard enough to love a thing, knowing you may lose it . . .
It is hopeless, when you know it will certainly be lost.

O not to the flutter of a heart whose rhythms bind me,
Knowing it will only beat awhile then fail when it must
To that cold ending that has haunted my faith in him
From the beginning . . . To love what flutters . . .
Men's hearts flutter, flutter . . . and fade.

Time-chained moments, impossible present-living,
Sterile tiresome heaven-love, flaw-blood of earthly passion . . .
Mortal love . . . give a name to it . . . Metamorphosis? . . .
Death-forgetting? . . . O they love, it seems,
What loves what flaws impair their loving . . .

Old moments shadow the new; they call that devotion . . .
The flowering of memory . . . how echoes wash the silent spaces
After the voices die . . . They dwell in former blisses;

He was Hyacinthos . . . I called him that;
O what a beautiful, beautiful child! He would have grown
To be a finer man! But . . . ah, there it is! There the flaw lies
Like a little thoughtless dishonesty lover-loosed

To animate his lovely . . . That love that shores itself
In moments' hoped-for continuation, always, always fails . . .
Will fail forever! . . . Until love's desire is either
Beaten to serenity or the heart perhaps learns
To love in a different way . . .

O why do we name things? What else do we give
But a lasting face to a looming permanent loss?

Why, why do we name things? Let us end
In calling them moments, and say
They are never the same.

II.

Heap of willow-limbs fallen, tangled supple boughs,
His whole creation tumbled derelict to the meadow . . .
No longer whole hale heart gashed, crown mutilated,
And temples ooze their naïve prayers-now-foul-effluvia . . .
His feather-veins flare through skin sheer gossamer,
Twisting him gaunt, inward drawn to a withered wasted
Snarled lifeless leaf that snaps into particles of dust, which,
Meadow-mingling, meld away . . .

Now comes that moment of utter aloneness,
Of disregard, abandonment, dereliction;
How swiftly leaving! leaving one not-long-desolate
Lonely with a freshly-devastated heart to writhe out the pain
Of love defeated, and faith wasted to a fruitless corpse . . .

His blood on the blades of the grassland
Still feebly drips a dying measure . . . failing, failing,
Failing to a far-severed thrum whose unions widen, widen,
Widen . . . and now, unexpected, so long coming after silence,
What could not be other than the final strum
Of soul to meadow sounds . . .

And maybe only once,
The earth for pity deigned
To couple with a plain-spoken life-song
Grief's groping-for-a-counterpart silent sad melody . . .

For a green head fumbles, flounders, feels fingers for the sun,
Rises unreasonably rare long limbs curling, leaping out of the earth;
And as I kneel beside this little lovely life-surge
The limbs erupt with flesh-white and eye-blue bird-like
Flowers, and seep a rarer flock of scattered beauteous birds
Hued like blood-and-bluedome-melded heliotrope
Lushly agleam below sun-loving leaves . . .

O indeterminate little flower, still twirling, shedding,
Putting forth his youthful pluck in petals radiant
From a sparrow-sweep of dawn- or dusk-voluptuousness!
You weep him away, branching, in little petals, little birds
That fall to other boughs, to other boughs, to other boughs . . .

O earth! . . . My thanks for this so sad and sweet consolation;
For nothing is blue as this is blue, as that *was* blue;
And nothing is white as this is white, as that *was* white;
And nothing mells so well his unresurrectable beauties . . .

O earth, who else, what else but you,
Can drink in a boy and exude a flower?

[Hylas]

To wake from dreams.

I stumble back, startled;
So intense a show of heavenly splendor
Overwhelming eyes unaccustomed
To sudden rays of unearthly light;
Nor have I earlier seen such beauty assembled,
Beauty seeming young like me, and yet, I know,
An illusion; perpetual youth countenanced alike
To freshness more common, which conventional youth in time
Collapses tangled, symmetry warped and nubility sunken,
Wasted by age.

First plea of the foremost:
Fair one, dawn being ablush,
'Tis evening, tho' still you breathe
The liquid fragrance of the breaking day;
Come lovely one, abide with us, - our buried abode
Houses pleasures undreamt of, unending indulgence,
Stainless gratification of the tender appetites,
Erogenous impulses, now furious, now unmet,
There satisfied by velvet divine . . .

First plea of the second:
Feel our perfect skin; the warmth,
The smallness of our hands;
Run your fingers through our hair,
Brush them over our eyes, along the satin ridges
Of our cheeks and delicate brows,
Kiss our rubicund lips,
Take our warm young bodies in your hands
And conquer us, - we yield;
Give yourself to us and we shall give you that
Which above all else, mortals wish for:
A heaven of pleasure, love, and play . . .

First plea of the last:
I feel a shiver flush my frame;
Cold water icing warm skin wakes delicate trembles;

My tresses sweep the bend of my lower back;
Flesh to flesh we too might heat each other through eternity;
You cannot hide it: you quiver, you yearn, you pine, you crave,
And maidens of the earth, were they even worthy of you,
Barely can keep their own selves warm through the rot
Of a hasty lifetime's falloff, so never can bear out your delectations;
See how the soft clear skin shivers . . . a caress will calm it,
Thaw it over you like a warm spring;
And it shall never fade away . . .

Quivering before their beauty, I thought,
How easy, dissipation, - to melt into
These fair girls' beckoning arms!
How easy, young life, to fall into the haven of Love,
To live embraced, bound by that embrace,
No longer fearful, having found an object
Worthy of devotion, worthy of worship,
Pleasantly supplanting the intricate hunt
For a greater, more harmonious passion!
O how often have I, knowing what I am,
Desired the embrace of a being as fair,
Yet knowing at once that she, my complement,
My dual, my opposite, must have in proportion
A total beauty not less, not greater,
Than that which I possess;
So does love become an aspiration
To which we settle not down nor compromise,
But by perfecting ourselves become more worthy
Of a companion more fair.

O how I hate the beautiful face
That does not appreciate itself,
Disingenuous veil of inward decay
Pretending to greater excellence, greater virtue, -
No villain more heinous to men and gods
Than he who being born to fairness
Degenerates his gift by the poverty of his choices,
Sinking himself to the station of a vile emblem,
Of symmetry self-shattered, and loveliness scorned.

But such uncertainty! Too much, I think, for the fledgling intellect,
Which always reckless, always uncertain, rather tends
To bend away from a beauty of action
That might have balanced the beauty of its form;
So we see the thoughtless lover disillusioned
By loves which seemed at first so satisfying,
But then, as they decay, wane to bitter from sweet.

Second plea of the foremost:
Many feel this: that love must decay;
That heaven is more than a private paradise,
And age will show how pleasure fades and lust alters
To a halcyon peacefulness of deep and absolute Love;
Many believe and say this. They lie. Truth is not resignation,
And the acceptance of a little earth to be the final
Bed of love, only delivers the heart
Whose creed is: Love must fade . . .

Second plea of the second:
What, fair one, more encompasses
Perennial everlastingness than this flesh
Of eternal flowerhood? All creation's floweriest
Moments of youth and beauty centered and preserved
In us, so made to give joy forever; for what higher charms
Can mingling make of flaws with fairnesses, mounting with
Failing with ideal elements, than the fulfillments we stand as?
That we desire you is enough. It is uncommon,
Spectacularly uncommon, for immortals to ask
For the company of men. Young men hate to die;
Old men consent because decrepitude
Has lowered them to it; eternally prime,
You shall not need those mortal salves . . .

Second plea of the last:
Has the earth, than me, produced a lovelier flower?
Tell me, if death and love cannot untwine,
Nor love be fully realized till that time
When moving rhythmically to the music
Of the moonlight, death's white flower
Dances to a dawn death in a dark bower . . .
All that twining and all that life

To flower for only a night?
And tell me, if you loved a maiden
And a maiden loved you, and the choice was given
To die or live together eternally in youth,
Would you choose to give over your love
To a dawn who'll ridicule a withered eternity
For choosing instead to be
A vain fleet flower?

Weak before their beauty, I thought,
Ah those lustrous eyes almost won me!
Those lustrous eyes beneath extravagant lashes
Gleaming . . . The warm flush of desire,
Of not only desiring but of being desired,
Dream of soft arms willing to enfold me;
Is this what love is? Is this what life?
Yet something in the subtle forces that lie below
The changes of life makes me pause at the brink of this
And shrink away from the immensity of endlessness;

I think perhaps they do not understand death,
And that is why they hate it, and tho' they offer mortal love
As merely a feebler analogue of their potential for devotion,
There is, I fear, in mortality something unfriendly
To the endlessly revolving stasis of eternity.

But O to feel the swell of apotheosis, to desire it,
To crown one's humanity with everlasting life,
Free from the fear of death, tho' human nonetheless,
Human till the close, feeling and thinking,
Loving . . . till love is no longer satisfying, nor ample,
To gratify the insatiable hollowness one inevitably feels
Thresholding, and yet excluded from, serene oblivion;
And to love is to persist in a middle state, -
Men love, and pass, glad for the pleasance
Of communal finitude, of shared collapse;
To live, living embraced, in the strong warmth
Of flesh that also fails, is to know
That love is marvelously pleasing;
Life lacking love, tho' short,
Becomes insufferable, forlorn slow extent

Of futile vanity, insincere endeavor,
Feigned indifference toward drifting lust, -
Human, though agonizingly contrary
To human variability, -

But if life must be lived,
And if to love is to live,
And if, even tho' to bear the frailties of a lover
Oftentimes may seem ignoble, it shall not seem that way
When in the end the sated heart accepts the death
That shall complete the arc that birth began;

I think that most dream not of infinite, but of lengthy life,
Of life which lasts until the joys we cannot bear to lose
Have lost their hold on us, and all of beauty and joy
Trails out of vibrant delight to a colorless indifference . . .
Could life be lived until each life were ready for death,
Then death would truly seem a part of life,
And not the destroyer of joys.

But now I feel the needle-tingle of desire in my blood;
The nascent winds gather; the time for sailing has approached;
I fall back on thoughts of the far-off ship,
The purple-breakered shore, the man I call father,
The men I call friends; but they only laugh,
Seize me with their swift hands,
And pull me beyond my will
Down into their darkness.

[Heracles]

Comfort in a night-bird.

Serene, then, as the sky and drifting stars,
As he took his life, he takes his death.
                         He leaves
Not unlike a bird that sings from tree to tree,
Unseen in the night, a melody that fades
As he departs away;
              We hear the psalm he sings,
And hear it soften as he goes,
Until at last his song has fully flown,
And then we sigh . . .

The one we never truly saw but knew
Only by the pleasant voice he gave the air,
Has carried off his song to other groves;
We sorrow, and the world seems less;
A tear for life's lyricism gone, for sweet tenor passing on,
For a tender sentiment withdrawn, and for our loss . . .
For it is the living who bear the forfeitures of the dead,
And we shall henceforth live only by remembrance,
And in tribute to our brothers gone away.

But there is one solace that rests in how the living go,
For like a singer singing as by darkness borne away,
We mourn him less and love him more
Who kindly flies the hearts of we
Who shall yet touch tomorrow's light of day,
Who for a moment loved his fluent lay,
And loved that when he went
He did not proudly fly a voiceless way,
Nor did he weep, but sang.

[Voice]

The Cuckoo. A solitary life estranged from joy.

Deep, O! Deep, O! Deep lover!
O deepest-loving lover of deepness,
Loving the depth she was, the depth she made of you;
O distraught! O lover-now-curser-of-love for making a deepness
To empty her out of, leaving you prisoner in a ditch,
Deep-ditch, girl-grave, gone; the girl goes
And you must stay - memory, love, hope - live on
Beyond her leaving, in the clutch of these no longer loved
But loving still, till in the end you follow.

Why, O! Why, O! Why love?
Why love what must let go, whether let go
Or not let go, what love one cannot make to last
As hope lasts, memory lasts, when to remember her
Will flush the fairmost to agony, fleeing fair - too fair -
To a dawn already past?

Now: release; release!
Life is, love is not released; she has, cannot be released;
Love, hope, memory, wound, bound to her, never to be
Twice found; for memory is not what love is,
Not soul enough to make love last, love live on;
Not giving-love-enough to keep her alive.

The soul is what the heart, to live, must lie to,
To love, must live for the fullness of the heart,
Blind, soul-blinding, heart-bleeding, blood of everything;

As nothing human is eternal, life must fade
To a soul weeping in a depth, must fade, soon or
Long off, life's beauty fade to a bleak leave-taking,
Melancholy not bare of a beauty of its own,
Struggling to the dawn of all love gave
Through the going dusk and the night
Of everything love could not give.

[Daidalos]

For to see a friend is grateful to the soul, come when he will.

Come, bright creatures, come down to us,
If you are not too light to fall . . .

You two eddying together, without crude arms
To force an embrace, weaving diaphanous bonds
Of colored light are blither symbols of human love
Than words can give wing to;

O spirit of the world outlying us,
Have you sent the day on wings to remind our captive hearts
Of the freedom and the loveliness of life without chains?
Or the world is mocking us, dipping its wings in this cave
That soddens our hearts that once were light as these . . .

O you sun-winged swallowtails dancing on the air,
How many flowers' fragile hearts have you kissed
To new life? We are two that might, unloved by you, fade,
Passed over by your tender touch, by your benevolence
That all bright things like you are bequeath
To the souls of all who gaze on you
And know they're not so free;

Icaros, they say these days
Earth's dark to love;
But see how much beauty still lives,
How much there is that does not die when times
Are cold to its delicacy, charm and grace, and will not pass on
To bleakness when love less honors it, and taste adores it less;
As always, my son, beauty in the world is timeless,
And as they live these two won't change
From what they are, and will never be
Less innocent, or less peaceful,
Or more cruel.

[Voices]

Songbirds. Bough-song hung upon a sleeping soul.

Elysium yawns beneath an oak bough,
Nods a wistful crown, and fresh heavens in the grass
Lay scattered round the dreamer; all the blisses
Seen and fancied crowd his brain,
And seem, together,
More than they were apart;

Heaven is not a place to be gone to,
But dwells instead in every heart.
Life is not a prelude, no, nor is life a great beginning,
And yet no eyes that grow to yearn for life
Find nothing in the world and in themselves
Of love and grace, and this they twine to;
And so the meadow wherefrom they die
Is the meadow they die into, and there-between they cast
The last long large look, lashes lovingly fall,
(They fall upon the light they love),
And as they end so end for them
Both love and light.

Here is no sad farewell;
Every hour remains of life before,
All is lived and cherished, and we shed no tears
For the days that never were;
We say: Perchance the sun may shine on the world
When I have gone from it; perchance the moon
Will glide the surface of the stars;
My hope is: *It shall be so.*
As for me they shone and wound my life
In ribbons of inspiring light, and drew
The beauties from the earth, which loveliness
Spilt forth to the sight of an admiring soul whose eyes
Could see and heart could know them lovely,
Imparting to my soul, as now to theirs,
The freedom of a heaven which is Human Love
Blushing through the prism of the world, -

So Love is a prelude,
And Love is a great beginning,
Not to any Paradise which turns the earth to nothing,
But to a dream which roots the end of our desires
Firmly in the fold of life and the world imperfect,
Rising when grief would kill men's faith
In the worth of love, vast solace to those whose hearts
Were bold enough to trust their bliss they know is frail
To the flaws they know impair the love of others;
And so Life becomes a song,
And the World is the music we sing to,
And death is never Death to him who carols Life
Until his voice fails and his heart beats out
The final rhythms; for he only finds
That not God without but God within him,
Confers upon the loves he holds the closest to his heart
The mortal kiss of Love Forever.

[Zeus]

God speaks to the child.

I.

O moon-fallen man, you think gods dream?
That to the calmer hours of eternal life they must
Genuflect still bodies to renew their spirits' zest?
Or that for weariness of troublous life they must retreat,
Infolding to the calm harbors of the mind
Where they may rest, breakered against the ocean of relentless life?
If as other men you dream that even gods live twice in a day,
You have not yet perceived our primary difference, -

Think how the line of days unbroken by reverie
Through the course of men's lives would bury the seeds
Of immortal nature within them; how the shoal logic they draw
From nature's circling echoes would narrow them
To a total worship of the observable world,
Rather than a worship of themselves, -

O to be a god is to believe
In the eternity of one's self, and the world men see
Beneath the sun is too bound to the rule of dawns and dusks
To grant to men even the slightest reasons for believing
That anything can truly last forever; and from their fears they devise
The most foolish paradises, that never truly resemble
The tragedies of their dreams, heavens of dull pleasure
That fail to reconcile mortal with immortal bliss, -

Gods love no time but the present, men love
No time but the past, and that is the sovereign order
Of their opposite raptures, - no beauty is better for men
Than that of the face that crowns the body of their memories,
While gods allow nothing of the past to taint their total love
Of the beauty of whatever touches them now . . .

Whatever you believe of gods' dalliance with men's adorations
Must echo from your human desire to fathom gods' hearts
In the hearts of men; but never will pure godliness

Become the azure road to any man's perfection,
And to a long-lived man the gods will show their contrast,
And he'll know that what men thought was godly
Was godly insofar as they intended to convey the opposite
Of what they appeared to express: that men's passions
Multiplied to eternity makes them nothing enduring,
Only snuffs them sooner to unmusicality when the mayhem
Of everything becoming permanent allows nothing to perish
That, opposed to reason, memory keeps stable; so madness,
When the mad ones become eternal, learns nothing,
Only grows hardier in folly, and suicidal in hysterical might.

II.

As nothing is before and nothing is beyond
A man's sole heart, authentic life indwells him;
Dreams, passions, truths, realized, reified,
Unfolding for his forever . . . It is men's passions
Not at the whim of the world, but the world at one soul's whim,
Distal soul, soul of the One Creature . . . Only He is uncreated,
Only He has come like a dream, emerging abstractly
To an abstract consciousness that subtlety cannot define,
Nor natural law limit, nor impermanence, nor mortality profane.

Dream on, then, of what you hold!
Blind wonderer, wanderer, rambler sad and yearning, -
If, to see the earth unbroken, heaven is the tower you need,
Then climb to whatever height can show you how ideal
Is one short life for the vague and wistful love
That you desire.

III.

For men are men because they desire
What they do not wish for, and what they
Would not love, were they given;
And love is love until it becomes an eternal springtime
And ceases to run away with loved meadows, and heap them back
When they are missed; and nothing is worthy of love and devotion
That will never diminish from a beauty eyes behold
To a beauty a heart is beholden to, which is no diminishment

But of watery semblance that ushers men's once-trite souls
To what they'll truly love when love's first springs dry,
And fades them flowering into unbeautiful old age,
That one life may seem to have given them nearly everything
Without taking too many things away;

There is chaos, and a wonderful disorder in dreams,
And that quality, vague as it must be, inspires renewal,
That by them men can accept the close of an existence
So long as memory will stay to console their hearts
At the end of life's short spring.

[Voice]

Thrush-song. Dream of an ideal ending.

Not for the frenzied moment kiss we now
To in a wolfish rush our tender bliss conclude,
Nor can we in our present joy conceive an end
To this our close embrace.

We two hearts in a world descending,
Beat forth our sovereignty over common snares;
The world may move, but we forever
Here beneath the bending moon may lay.

The world, the world will never know,
Will never know the romance here begun;

The fire, the fire suspended here
As here we bleed our love away
Before the dawning sun.

[Endymion]

The Asphodel Meadows.

O pale asphodel, are you a dream?
Pale, pale, pale flower, bloodless among
Your brothers, stand motionless in the meadow,
The still, the white, the silent meadow;

How frail is heaven among the others!
How much a prison they make of everything,
Even of love, even of faith, even of desire!
In life they sleep like asphodels in the meadow;
In death they sleep like asphodels in the meadow;
They ask nothing more than to flower in a meadow,
Wave in a meadow, die in a meadow; they receive
Nothing more than the meadow they desire;

Forgetfulness sustains us best, yes, and a few tears
To carry us under,
          They say.

[Zeus]

Tartaros. Though an unreal vision of the night.

These are the murmurs of the measureless departed,
The drone of the earth, the babble of buried beings;
True worlds cannot suffer much, soon give way to despair,
Soon slip sadly into nothingness, soul's anarchy,
And the sweetness of life is nothing but the crumble to death;

Sleep frees you, - breaks the balance, the unity of things,
Loosens faith, firmness, certainty, inevitability,
Leaving only a vague familiarness to keep you
Bound to yourself; and to wake is merely to find firm ground,
Reemerge to a level of trust with the universe;

O sleep forever, lonely child, and even the joy of freedom
Will some day perish in the overflow! Spurn them, call them
Petty and trivial, those little lovelinesses the living live for,
So long as your desires are not truly the same, -
For never think yourself free of anything
If your freedom is merely a convolution
Of what others declare in a simpler way . . .

Sweet sleep ripples over the mind,
Bathes a heart in fair and frightening visions,
Takes you away from the meaningless mores of life,
Labors of living, - and however sweet this is for a moment,
The sweetness comes from the departure;
Nothing to leave, nothing to reemerge to,
And there will fade the great divergence
Of body and mind, earth and heaven,
Life and death into their own elements,
Mingle them together to a bland colorlessness
That ceases to delight, but cannot be departed from;

Earth and heaven shine for the living,
Earth in sight and heaven in thought;
Like pure love love they, and they are loved
As only life itself inspires love and adoration . . .

The unity of the dead, how all lives end
And join the thoughtless drift
To the other side of eternity;
That drift felt only by the living,
Great meaningless unfathomably endless
Advance toward nothing, the dead
Having already arrived there
On the wind of their ending breaths . . .

Frail man, what do you wish for?
The high sun dies now to the dim plain;
You ask if gods dream?

      Yes, they dream;
      But they only dream.

[Endymion]

Thánatos.

I have . . .
I have seen him, Death,
And he is a lovely pale youth,
Have seen how nightly he, wide eyes
Of frosted starlight, leaves his cave
When the pure moon shines, to hunt
For butterflies in the dove-gray darkness;
Have seen how, oddly, he bears a torch not aburn with flames,
But barely ember-blooming tiny flares like sweet alyssum
Flowering sallow small flowerets along short shoots;
And how absolutely silently he lurks, prowls,
Barely more than a thin shadow, stalks
The flicker of his object's eyelid-flutter
Winking among the colonnaded
              Moonbeams . . .

              He follows,
Smoothly like the very shade
His focus casts, advancing deliberately,
Gradually . . . Till throwing out a long,
Ivory-fingered hand, he ends his victim's motions,
Snares him in a five-columned curled pearl cage
Wherein the creature yet shudders his sheer wings uselessly . . .

And bearing his victim delicately, whispers
Something valerian to the creature, who then subsides,
Quietens, unruffles all fear-tension, sinks slack wings
Serenely; then slipping back through shadows with his prize
Death flees, poppy-wreathed, bloodless, sliding silently
Through the catacombs of the night, flees to the yawn
Of his gloom-draped cavern . . .

And at the mouth thereof, douses in the dust
His torch's last frail embers . . . They smoke,
And the smoke and the darkness dissolve him.

I have seen him hunt many a winged soul,
And always he takes them below, always he rises
Alone; I think he loves their delicateness;
Loves how, innocently, they wander, willingly,
They acquiesce, how graceful he must be
Not to break them when he plucks them,
Nor when he bears them, slumbrous,
Out of the free starlight to the swathing darkness
Of his tranquil home under the world, where, I deem,
He shelves them somewhere in the perfect night,
Saving them (he must dream) from their labor
Of incessant fluttering . . .

It is difficult to say
Whether he hates
Or loves them.

[Endymion]

Hypnos.

I have . . .
I have seen him, Sleep,
And he is a lovely pale youth,
Have seen the poppies about his cavern,
The fall beyond them almost imperceptibly
Into darkness, the sleepy hum of his grotto,
The drowsing king of dreams . . .

I woke upon a stream, woke to find myself
Borne down the current in the night, the gleaming
Tree-shadows vaulting into star-chambers, the heavy
Darkness weaving bole, bough, over and undergrowth
On bank and bank to a deeper and denser texture
As I floated, limb-numb, down the river's dwindling
Murmur-mutter-mumble-babble-ripple-plashing
Silver course, till raw lips looming of a vast mouth
Rose and drank us into black bowels . . .

He is an indolent king, rarely more
Than between-dreams fluttering his eyes, -
And they glint in the gloom, those eyes
Filled with the fire of infinite dreams,
Glint as he nearly-but-never-fully wakes;
O and he is flushed, flushed with joy!
It is clear he is touched by little or nothing of the world,
So has been forever; and I wonder: then of what does he dream?

I have seen him in the half-light
Take mallet and gouge to a living writhing beast
And shape it without pain into something new;
Eyes like embers abloom, he wakes,
He wavers on life's shores . . . Then lets them
Fall with a flutter to the pathless loveliness
Of his own heart's creation . . .

I saw him once emerge from his cavern to the night,
Either it was he or it was a butterfly, I saw something

Either drink or wreath itself with blood-red night-black
Flowers, then seemingly dissolve into nothingness . . .
How can one describe him? He can be many things at once,
And none of them expected . . . Now he slumbers in the fold
Of gauzy curtains, rustling their vague drapery now and then
When a little light or language leaps off him . . . Or is he there,
Bending those liquid thoughts into golden birds or
Massive misshapen men, or other things beautiful, bizarre,
Grotesque? . . . No, no, it cannot be,
For see how he sleeps . . .

And I, I woke upon a stream,
And rode those waters very very deep
Into the foundations of the earth . . . My memory
Serves me faintly of this voyage, yet brings me feelings
Of a wild river slackening lethargically
Into languor, of dark translucent barely-moving waters
Buoying me to a smooth shore . . . And yonder
Of a dark slumberer, throned on his sable-feathered
Berth, corpselike lying wan-moon-lustrous like one lone light
Shimmering upon a sea-mists'-gloom-enfolded isle . . .
And there on the bank I saw the bodies drifting past
His place of slumber, saw them sucked through still air
Like ribbons of themselves spun to bird flight
They rose in luminous flurries of flesh-become-fluid
And shot through him as he rested . . . And O he was kinetic
Even in his slumber! At once at rest, at once at fabrication,
How he wrung and wrestled with them as they passed!
Those blustery traversers come from earth
To the realm of dreams, how he hammered them
Into startling forms, unexpected structures,
Disquieting configurations . . .

It is difficult to say
Whether he hates
Or loves them.

[Heracles]

The Golden Cup of the Sun.

What if a golden vessel carried the sun
From his dusk to his dawn?
And what if he were something like a man,
But greater of body, of beauty, of radiant light
Off skin and hair, welling out of his eyes?
And what if, infolded to the night, he rode the quiet ocean,
Ship of golden air, slumbering below the bell
Of a silver sail, to the threshold's blush of Dawn's
So-youthful loveliness, to chase her dreamily into the sky?
Till she vanishes as he awakens, and he, remembering her vaguely
As a thing worth chasing tremendously far into heaven,
Pursues on, till empty depths and his own heart's heaviness
Carry him, melancholy, down to his rest
Beyond the mountains and the trees;
And what if a man were to feel the falling shafts
Of the lusty climbing lover the sun, and rage thereunder,
Angered by the heavy stab of so-bold spears, and set his anger
To a string, and aim that arrow against heaven's light?
And what if the sun admired his small-man's boldness,
And spoke to him, praising a little thing for defying a large?

There is the vessel, he said, it will take you against the wind.
I embarked, and the wind seemed nothing to me,
One foot to the golden deck and a vision of what I sail to;
And then darkness and the forest.

Truly, glances of a hope beyond reason
Are the most to part with, granting the sight
Of a gracious Sun, only to wake us to a dim evening
Where somewhere far away the sun is slumbering,
Infolded to the gifts he gave
And did not give.

[Daidalos]

Islands of the Blest.

Men of a golden age, whose only thought
Was happiness, feasted on the pleasures of life and youth
Till sleep, warm tide, came over them, then fell to fair dreams
And that was death. This open-hearted race has long since gone,
But still persists in what men innocently do
In pursuit of the joys of life.

Icaros, what do you think is joy? What is heaven?
What would you have, could anything be given?
Or has there been not daylight enough in your young sad life
For wistful retracings, to make them behind you leap ahead?
Yet still you knew a life before this, and, as I remember,
Some share of happiness possessed, may still posses
There in some warm corner of your heart; I love that
Wonder that you are, that dawn on the water,
Anticipating what comes next;

Yet how you know, I know not, nor know how multiplies
That nameless flame I seem to see in your eyes, strange, indefinite,
Virgin, that so distinctly fans to ardor these embers
You perfectly trust never to peter out to dreamless ashes,
No more to arc with glints of fire, sporing blazes
On the bright winds;

Thus you are, that I less dwindle
In the half-light, having a sun below me,
Streamer of that faith that strangely comes
When another's seamless love accepts as true
What we doubt within ourselves.

[Admetos]

The flow'ry wreath, and song that used to echo through my house.

Once I told her of a dream, as we lay folded
In the light of morning, told I between soft kisses,
My love what dream the night had shown me:

I saw a mist among leaves,
Dawn mist, that gives a body to the light
And lets the low sun pierce the dewy woodland's
Virescent columns and climbing walls
As they emerge out of the valleys of the night; I saw
Your wedding white, the robes of lily-white you wore
When songs of union rolled us to our bliss; I saw
No body, but heard your voice, and you were saying
What once I heard you say:
No wealth's intricate gift,
Nor song of love or wisdom,
Shall I ever love or heed so much
As a bird calling at the window.

And there was the feeling among these words
Of moving through a portal that framed
The fresh and leafing and dewy-eyed unwilting world;
There rose the singing of many birds, and the portal scattered, -
'Twas not the sun-glowing world, but their bright wings
Mosaicing, and tho' began their many songs in disarray,
Gradually they fell together, as tones align to melody,
And drew they from their flights together again and their song
Was our wedding song and their portal yon portal
That opens from our wedding chamber to the world.

And it was that morning when by the clear sun-bright waters
We washed away the impurities of our prior lives
To the greater love and suffering of the next;
We bathed that day apart, and yet I could not say
Who I saw emerge at the water's edge, nor how
The massive waters of the lake seemed then no different
Than the caught showers pooled in the thousand
Natural basins of a crimson-berried tree

Wherebeneath we stood; and there was a bird
Calling out above us, no birdsong but your voice saying,
No wealth's intricate gift,
Nor song of love or wisdom,
Shall I ever love or heed so much
As a bird calling at the window.

And I looked to the so-loved green of your eyes,
And the twin bright orbs there hung so warm and lovely;
But as if I could not well remember your face
I saw you only as a thing of white, and hardly could know
That you were you but that I could perceive within some curve
Of shape and color, some doubt of fluid form,
Some lilt of things around me, your nature's contours,
That grace that is all of you, compounded as a year of seasons
Mingles to the delights one had of each,
And only the strongest go on . . .

And there I ended, saying the dream trailed off
To nothing; And yet I should have gone on
To tell my lovely girl the moods my dream
Trailed off to, for I might have said,

And there without you, yet in the midst of you,
Amid the movements of the eye and the ear and the heart
That involve us, that somehow indicate what you are
To what I am, implying Love as that thing between us,
That thing binding us, and I recall the overwhelming feeling
Of Time's passage, as tho' long days were rolling over my eyes,
Long long days condensed to a melody or a wingbeat
Or a hope or a touch or a sigh, days bright with purpose,
Unselfish days, life primarily lived for another soul,
A soul when together with mine, missing nothing,
My soul, wound with yours, missing nothing, no more
Shame or semblance or lonely bitterness or timid pusillanimity,
No longer quivering at the thought of never being loved,
But magnified to a harmony of spirit that only finds
Joy endless and peace limitless in the mystery of another's love for us,
And in how much we gain and how much we sacrifice
To return their love, and how our love is only as deep
As our hope that heaven embraces them when we embrace them,

And like God granting the sight of grace we make love pour
From all the fountains of the earth for them, and cherish them
So truly and completely that they offer us their heart's short season of life
And vine their heart inseparably around our heart and trust us
To love them and not to destroy them, and desire no gifts from us
Except for a devoted heart to think of holding them
When a bird comes calling at the window.

[Daidalos]

There await me till I die.

The rain will fall, will fall fragrant,
Will fall on the fragrant sea . . .

      . . . We love ourselves
Only to the trembling margin of loneliness,
Never to launch distinct selves shivered free
Of the bonds of affection and obligation
To split the silver sea-dawn onward
And never let our eyes follow our heart
To the wake we widen behind us . . .

The sea has a dim memory, never suffering
From the hauntings of passions retraced and loves revived,
Ringing with brief nostalgia of echoes
Until lapsing into blank vacancy,
Broken with the past, -
Nothing is remembered, nothing misremembered,
Nothing reverenced, nothing disregarded,
Nothing is forgotten or left behind,
And nothing is reprised but oscillation;
But that is not the will of the sea,
Only the sea's reaction.

Think of me, you echoes, as you go heedlessly to oblivion,
And think how 'tis best we live shortly,
Being unable to forget;

And how, from our beginnings,
We spread to our ends.

[Icaros]

Then bid excessive grief farewell . . .

Like a falcon to plummet
Through alps of mist and towering clouds;
Or kestrel-like to hover against the wind
And fall thereafter; or swallow-like to swoop
And skim the waters when they steam
With beautiful vapor; or kite-like widening
The broad fingers of my wings slip alongside
The sprightly gusts, riding them to heaven . . .

O to fade forever into dreams of this
With open eyes! The sweep of this, this freedom!
This dream . . . O how can I fall from this dream?
This dream, this dream, the only dream
I need not fall from . . . For if I
Fall, all of this, all, all of this . . .
The earth I flee, the heaven I flee to . . .
If what I know is all I know . . .
All falls with me.

[Endymion]

And visiting my dreams, delight me.

It is: farewell.
Farewell to everything!
          And that is death;
Farewell to one loved thing,
To another,
                    And that is life;
Farewell to the woods and the stars,
To the hills of wandering;
Farewell to the sunset dawns, violaceous,
To the cerise incipience of slumber;
Farewell to the dread of a world's intrusion,
And farewell most of all to you, my love . . .

My love, my love, our dreams dissolve to a life
That holds me a heaven away from you;
I shall chase you deeply, then, deeply into the dreams
Our passions stem from, and soon my eyes
Will rise to find your eyes;

Often I have thought that if I must die
I would die lost in the pathless loveliness
Of some fantasy of life; so shall I live;
Truly, it is the only way;
I have held my solitude long enough;
Soon the world will find me,
And our love cannot abide that;

Here the fountain breaks earth open;
Here I lie on the margin, and God has lately
Whispered in my ear the promise
Of eternal life, eternal slumber;
I need no longer hide
From the harsh music
Of the dawn;
Now, at last,
I can rest.

A numbness comes through me now,
Slowly, like a tender lowering
Into balmy currents, and the world
Rolls back now like a curtain thrown aside
By one great flood of wind,
And everything falls away now
From a low portion of the sky
Where you, my love, now hang
The camber of your loveliness . . .

And you eddy, my love, you eddy
To an orb now, now to an eye,
To a pure gray eye . . .

O how is to wake . . .
O how is to wake from dreams
To return to life?
I need no other, no other
Lips . . . only your
Perennial
Love.

Farewell to Spring

8941908R0

Made in the USA
Charleston, SC
28 July 2011